nourished beginnings
baby food

nourished beginnings
baby food

Nutrient-Dense Recipes for Infants, Toddlers and Beyond
Inspired by Ancient Wisdom and Traditional Foods

WITHDRAWN

renee kohley
founder of Raising Generation Nourished

PAGE STREET
PUBLISHING CO.

PAGE STREET
PUBLISHING CO.

Copyright © 2016 Renee Kohley

First published in 2016 by

Page Street Publishing Co.

27 Congress Street, Suite 103

Salem, MA 01970

www.pagestreetpublishing.com

Distributed by Macmillan, sales in Canada by The Canadian Manda Group.

19 18 17 16   1 2 3 4 5

ISBN-13: 978-1-62414-301-4

ISBN-10: 1-62414-301-6

Library of Congress Control Number: 2016937970

Cover and book design by Page Street Publishing Co.

Photography by Jade Gedeon

Author photo by Jill Burrows Photography

Printed and bound in China

dedication

To my 3 little ladies, who have captured my heart
and given me a passion.

Love, Momma

contents

introduction

There is something powerful about food and the company we share it with.

From as far back as we have recorded time, we see that food brings people together. It creates community, comfort and enjoyment.

Somehow, as time has passed, modern society has slowly taken a toll on how we look at food. Cooking has become a cumbersome task that takes time away from our busy schedule. We have birthed a generation of children who have lost the art of slowing down to create and eat a meal together.

The rise of the real-food movement, however, is changing the way we look at food. More and more people are asking great questions like, "Where did this food come from?" and "Would my great-grandparents have eaten food like this?" We are seeing with our own eyes the impact that processed food is making on a generation of children, and many people are standing up to make the processed-food trend a thing of the past.

But where do we begin?

When all you have ever known is food from a box, where do you even start?

This was me. That was my question 10 years ago when I started my real food journey.

It would be a few more years before I had kids of my own, but as a newlywed in my own home I could see how the habits we formed growing up stuck with us through adulthood. It was hard for me to try new foods. It was hard to serve my husband vegetables he had never had before. It was hard to learn how to cook … and I wanted it to be different for my own kids.

When I got back to the basics and really became interested in how my great-grandparents would have eaten, it became clearer. My great-grandma would have nursed her babies, and when they were ready, they would have eaten from the table that the family was sitting around. Plain and simple. There were no toddler puffs, baby cereals or brightly colored "kid foods." These were generations that sat around the dinner table and everyone ate the same thing.

And when I researched further, back to what healthy traditional peoples would have been eating, it became clear that the focus was on nutrient-dense food from the land they were living on. They would have eaten meat and seafood from the area in which they lived. Mothers would pre-chew sacred, nutrient-dense foods like livers for their babies to eat as their "first foods." They instinctively knew the nutritional benefits of how they fed their babies and passed these traditions down through each generation.

When I became a parent, I wanted to give my kids the best start I could. I wanted them to have a broader taste palate than I had—and I wanted them to enjoy real food. Because I was working a lot when I had my first baby, I didn't have time to create elaborate separate meals for her that fit my nourishing food goals. When we were ready to start solids with her, my husband and I finally jumped (with both feet) into eating real food. One meal; everyone shared. We sat around the table as much as we could with our busy schedules and everyone ate the same thing. Baby's food would be adjusted to her needs by mashing or blending the food (think traditional people's pre-chewing), and that was that.

It was a relief! I could cook for my whole family at the same time. To this day, as I now have 7-, 5- and 3-year-olds, we eat at a family table. All food at our house is kid food. It is family food.

I want to bring this to your home. You will create broad taste palates in your little ones so that they don't bat an eye at being served a plate of meat and vegetables, and light up at their favorite meal. You can make meal time a delight instead of a chore. And most importantly, you will be nourishing your family. We have a generation of children who have full plates but their bodies are literally starving for nutrients of real food that will make their bodies function right. You can raise a different generation, one that knows where its food comes from, and how it affects the body, one that has healed guts, functioning minds and solid health.

It all starts at the beginning. If you have babies ready to start solids at home, you can give them a nourished beginning. You will be rewarded with a child who is nourished from the inside out, one who is an adventurous eater as a toddler and big kid and truly enjoys sitting down at the table with the family to share a meal.

a quick note: if you already have toddlers and big kids at home who have their minds made up about what food they like and dislike, this book is for you, too. Take some baby steps. Start with making one meal a day a real-food meal, or something they haven't tried before. You really can still transform those taste palates from craving processed food to craving real food. Slowly transition the kitchen away from housing the processed food. If it isn't there, it won't get eaten.

Renee Kohley

how to use this book & tips for feeding babies

First and foremost, always keep in mind that every baby is different. Their metabolisms are different, families have different schedules, eating times and traditions for what meals are "lighter" and what meals are "heavier." And since every family has kids of different ages (who are ever-growing and have shifting appetites), serving sizes will be different for each member of the family. These recipes are meant to be your inspiration. What I love about my blogging job is getting to meet people from all over the world and learning about the food from their culture. This book represents food that is available where I live and in many parts of the world. However, if, in your family, for instance, lamb is more accessible than it is where I live, substitute lamb for some of the other meat! If you use certain seasonings and spices in your cultural cooking, get baby's palate used to that.

Serving sizes for baby should follow baby's lead. Start with a tablespoon (15 ml) as a serving size and see if that is sufficient. It is pretty hard to overfeed a baby. When babies are done eating, they shift in their seats, turn their heads or become uninterested or fuss. End the meal when baby is ready—even if it has just been a couple of spoonfuls. If the baby is leaning in for more after you finish a tablespoon (15 ml), by all means try another spoonful. If you find that baby is spitting up after a meal, he or she may have eaten too fast and/or too much, so you can slow it down next time. Also keep in mind that if baby is extra fussy, gassy, has projectile vomiting or has visible redness anywhere around the mouth after the introduction of a food, those can be signs of sensitivity to that food. Stop that food for a month or two before trying it again.

Keep the texture of baby's food as close to the real thing as possible. Making baby's food super runny and thin for everything will teach baby that food always has the same texture. Smooth it out in the beginning while the baby learns how to manage the food in his or her mouth, but you will find you won't have to do this for very long. Every baby develops differently, but somewhere between 6 months to a year, babies will be able to manage "finger food" style prep in which you can just cut the soft food into bite-sized pieces for them to manage themselves.

Keep in mind that it can take baby up to 15 attempts at trying a new food to accept it. If she or he isn't interested at first, don't give up! Try again the next day, and if it is still a no-go, then pop the food into the freezer to try again next week! I can't tell you how many times I got turned-up noses at new tastes only to have them gobble that food down a month later.

My final thought here is to enjoy this season. I truly miss this part of raising my babies! Feeding baby should be a fun, positive experience. Baby will pick up your positive (or negative) attitude toward food and that is a promise. Babies will feel it when you are hesitant about whether or not they will like the food. Remember, a baby is a blank slate, with zero past experience to draw from! When babies see you smiling and enjoying the food as well while you feed them, they will too.

part 1

simple starts for baby

The recipes here are the basic food introductions for babies 5-9 months who are new to solids. These foods will set the stage for creating a broad taste palate for baby to create an adventurous, well-rounded eater.

The goal in this section is not to overwhelm yourself with a lot of time spent preparing baby food to store and freeze away. Rather, plan your family meals and make baby a part of it! If the family dinner will be roast beef, green beans and sweet potatoes, then baby can have forms of this meal blended up a little or pureed. This means less baby-food planning, and more making baby a part of the family table. You will learn how to nourish your baby with nutrient-dense foods like grass-fed liver that have been used for generations, how to prepare yolks from pastured hens for brain-building food, and how to create a love for vegetables right from the earliest of ages.

chapter 1

vegetable purees

Introducing a variety of vegetable flavors, colors and textures will pave the way to having toddlers and school-aged children who won't fight about those green beans you put on their plate. Vegetables are so rich in vitamins and minerals and are a fantastic component to just about every meal baby eats. And since vegetables are on everyone's plate in the family, preparing baby's vegetables will go right alongside making your dinner.

All vegetables in this section are pureed with water or bone broth. Use what you have on hand. You can find my recipe for bone broth on page 184. Bone broth adds extra nourishment to the meal as well as makes it taste really good. There are tips in the broth recipes for making bone broth a quick process that can fit into anyone's schedule so it is always on hand. You will also notice that each recipe in this section incorporates a "friendly fat" with each vegetable. Vegetables are digested best with a little nourishing fat, and the vitamins in the veggies are best absorbed with the fat. You can follow each recipe as it's written, or switch up the fats depending on what you have available. There are many benefits to each individual fat source, so changing it up and rotating things is a good idea. There is a list of friendly fats that are safe to use, as well as fats to avoid, on page 193.

peas with bone broth, butter and sea salt

Bright, fresh peas will become one of baby's favorite finger foods as a toddler when you start with a mashed pea meal they love! Peas are a great source of vegetable protein, vitamins and minerals. When peas cook down in the butter and sea salt, they become sweet—especially to baby's sensitive palate! The friendly fat in the butter will help the peas to be easily digested and will help baby's digestive system absorb the fat-soluble vitamins.

Peas, fresh or frozen

Splashes of water or bone broth (see bone broth recipe on page 184)

Butter

Sea salt

steaming method

Steam the fresh or frozen peas in your steamer for 15 minutes. If you are using frozen peas, you don't even have to thaw them; just dump them into the steamer right from the freezer! Blend to puree, adding splashes of water or bone broth to get the desired texture. You can use a food processor or blender.

pan-sauté method

Warm your pan over medium heat, add 2 to 3 tablespoons (30 to 45 g) of butter to melt per 2 cups (268 g) of peas, and then add the peas with a few pinches of sea salt. If you are using frozen peas, you can add them to the pan right from the freezer; no need to thaw! You can cook more than 2 cups (268 g) at a time if you plan to freeze for later use.

Cook the peas over medium heat until they are bright green and softened, about 5 minutes. Pour the peas into your blender or food processor, including the cooking fat left in the pan, and puree until smooth. Thin the puree with water or bone broth to your baby's liking.

When serving baby, start with a tablespoon (15 ml) of pea puree, and add a teaspoon of butter along with a pinch of sea salt to the puree and stir to combine.

Leftovers from either method can be kept in the fridge for about 5 days, or can be frozen for months in ice cube trays for baby servings or freezer-safe containers for larger servings.

carrots with tallow or lard and sea salt

Baby is going to love these sweet little carrots! Not only are carrots filled with vitamins, minerals and antioxidants, the tallow and sea salt add an extra vitamin and mineral punch, too. The friendly fats in the tallow will help baby digest these carrots easily, as well as help her digestive system absorb the fat-soluble vitamins.

This is about as easy as it gets, too. If you are planning on carrots with your dinner, you can steam or pan sauté carrots for the whole family, and scoop some out to puree for baby! No extra cooking or special foods here.

Carrots

Splash of water or bone broth
(see bone broth recipe on page 184)

Lard or tallow (see recipe for rendering
lard & tallow on page 187)

Sea salt

steaming method

Steam the carrots (you don't even have to chop them!) in your steamer for 30 minutes, and then blend to puree, using a food processor or blender. You can add a splash of water or bone broth to thin, if needed, to baby's liking.

pan-sauté method

Cut the carrots into "coins." Warm your pan over medium heat, add 2 to 3 tablespoons (25 to 38 g) of lard or tallow to melt per 2 cups (244 g) of carrots, and then add the carrots with a few pinches of sea salt. You can cook more than 2 cups (244 g) at a time if you plan to freeze for later use.

Cook the carrots over medium heat until they are bright orange and fork-tender, about 7 to 10 minutes. Pour the carrots into your blender or food processor, including the cooking fat left in the pan, and puree until smooth. You can thin the puree with water or bone broth if needed.

When serving baby, start with a tablespoon (15 ml) of carrot puree, add a teaspoon of lard or tallow along with a pinch of sea salt and stir to combine.

Leftovers from either method can be kept in the fridge for about 5 days, or can be frozen for months in ice cube trays for baby servings or freezer-safe containers for larger servings.

zucchini and marrow with bone broth and sea salt

Zucchini is a fun summer staple in our home that my girls have come to look forward to every June. When babies have had zucchini from babyhood, they really come to love them!

Zucchini and marrow go well together because the high fat content in the marrow will allow the fat-soluble vitamins, like vitamin K in the zucchini, to be absorbed. Zucchini is also a great source of many minerals including magnesium, potassium and natural sodium, all of which nourish our adrenals and electrolyte balance.

Zucchini

Splashes of water or bone broth (see bone broth recipe on page 184)

Marrow from cooked pastured beef bones (see directions for roasting marrow bones in the bone broth recipe on page 184)

Sea salt

steaming method

Slice the zucchini into ½-inch (1.3-cm) rounds. Steam the zucchini in your steamer for 15 minutes. Blend the cooked zucchini along with 2 tablespoons (25 g) marrow per 2 cups (226 g) of zucchini in your food processor or blender. Add pinches of sea salt to taste when serving.

pan-sauté method

Slice the zucchini into ½-inch (1.3-cm) rounds. Warm your pan over medium heat, add 2 tablespoons (25 g) of marrow to melt per 2 cups (226 g) of zucchini, and then add the zucchini with a few pinches of sea salt. You can cook more than 2 cups (226 g) at a time if you plan to freeze some for later use.

Cook the zucchini over medium heat until the skin turns bright green and the zucchini has softened, about 7 to 10 minutes. Pour the zucchini into your blender or food processor, including the cooking fat left in the pan, and puree until smooth. Thin the puree with water or bone broth to your baby's liking.

When serving baby, start with a tablespoon (15 ml) of zucchini puree, and add a teaspoon of marrow along with a pinch of sea salt and stir to combine.

Leftovers from either method can be kept in the fridge for about 5 days, or can be frozen for months in ice cube trays for baby servings or freezer-safe containers for larger servings.

broccoli and coconut oil with bone broth and sea salt

Antioxidant-rich broccoli is a weekly staple at our table, and there is no forcing these nutritious vegetables when you start introducing them in babyhood with yummy, sweet coconut oil!

Coconut oil is rich in lauric acid, almost identical to the lauric acid found in breast milk that helps to protect the immune system. The friendly fat in the coconut oil will help the broccoli be digested easily as well as help baby's digestive system absorb the fat-soluble vitamins.

Broccoli florets, fresh or frozen

Splashes of water or bone broth
(see bone broth recipe on page 184)

Coconut oil

Sea salt

steaming method

Steam the broccoli in your steamer for 25 minutes. If you are using frozen broccoli, you don't even have to thaw it! Just dump the florets into the steamer right from the freezer. Blend to puree, adding splashes of water or bone broth to make the texture the way you want it. You can use a food processor or blender.

pan-sauté method

Warm your pan over medium heat, add 2 to 3 tablespoons (25 to 38 g) of coconut oil to melt per 2 cups (182 g) of broccoli, and then add the broccoli with a few pinches of sea salt. If you are using frozen broccoli, this method works best if the broccoli is thawed first. You can cook more than 2 cups (182 g) at a time if you plan to freeze some for later use.

Cook the broccoli over medium heat until it is bright green and softened, about 15 to 20 minutes. Pour the broccoli into your blender or food processor, including the cooking fat left in the pan, and puree until smooth. Thin the puree out with water or bone broth to your baby's liking.

When serving baby, start with a tablespoon (15 ml) of broccoli puree, and add a teaspoon of coconut oil along with a pinch of sea salt and stir to combine.

Leftovers from either method can be kept in the fridge for about 5 days, or can be frozen for months in ice cube trays for baby servings or freezer-safe containers for larger servings.

squash with butter and kraut juice

This meal with sweet squash, creamy butter and sea-salty kraut juice is filled with delicious flavor and texture for baby, and is loaded with nutrients.

Not only is squash high in vitamins and minerals, adding the probiotic-rich punch of kraut juice will nourish baby's tummy flora for healthy digestion and a powerful immune system. Simply scoop the juice from a jar of sauerkraut right into the puree. Squash is very simple to digest, and the friendly fat in the butter will help baby's digestive system absorb the fat-soluble vitamins in the squash.

Winter squash such as butternut, acorn, kobucha or buttercup, halved with seeds scooped out

3 tbsp (45 g) butter, plus more for serving

1 tsp sea salt

$\frac{1}{4}$ tsp kraut juice per tablespoon (15 ml) squash puree

Preheat the oven to 425°F (220°C).

Put the halved squashes flesh-side up on a baking sheet, butter the flesh and sprinkle with the sea salt.

Roast at 425°F (220°C) for 50 to 60 minutes. When ready, the flesh should be fork-tender and have a caramelized look.

Scoop the cooked squash into your blender or food processor and puree. You can add a splash or two of water or bone broth to thin it out if you need to for baby.

When serving, add $\frac{1}{4}$ teaspoon kraut juice per tablespoon (15 ml) of squash puree for baby, along with a $\frac{1}{2}$ teaspoon of butter. The kraut juice should give enough salt taste but you can add sea salt to taste if you wish.

Leftovers can be kept in the fridge for about 5 days, or can be frozen for months in ice cube trays for baby servings or in freezer-safe containers for larger servings.

note: As baby gets older and wants to eat with his fingers, you can skin the squash, cube it and roast it by the same method for about 40 minutes. Squash cubes are so sweet, and my babies ate them like candy!

green beans with whole yogurt and sea salt

One of my favorite times of the year is midsummer, when I take my girls through the garden and watch them gobble up fresh green beans right off the bush. It blows me away every time they are so enthusiastic about eating them, but the green bean flavor has been with them since babyhood. They really developed a taste for them and now they love them!

Green beans sweeten a little when you cook them, and pairing them with tangy, whole plain yogurt is a great combination. Getting your baby used to the tang of a plain yogurt will reward you with a baby who is accustomed to it and who doesn't need to have sugar-laden commercial yogurts to get a cup down.

Green beans, fresh or frozen

Splashes of water or bone broth (see bone broth recipe on page 184)

Whole unsweetened plain yogurt

Butter, for cooking with the sauté method

Sea salt

steaming method

Steam the green beans in your steamer for 25 minutes. If you are using frozen green beans, you don't even have to thaw them! Just dump them into the steamer right from the freezer. Blend to puree, adding splashes of water or bone broth to make the texture the way you want it. You can use a food processor or blender.

pan-sauté method

Warm your pan over medium heat, add 2 tablespoons (25 g) of butter to melt per 2 cups (220 g) of green beans, and then add the green beans with a few pinches of sea salt. If you are using frozen green beans, this method works best if the green beans are thawed first. You can cook more than 2 cups (220 g) at a time if you plan to freeze some for later use.

Cook the green beans over medium heat until they are bright green and softened, about 15 minutes. Pour the green beans into your blender or food processor, including the cooking fat left in the pan, and puree until smooth. Thin the puree out with water or bone broth to your baby's liking.

When serving baby, start with a tablespoon (15 ml) of green bean puree, and add a teaspoon of yogurt along with a pinch of sea salt and stir to combine.

Leftovers from either method can be kept in the fridge for about 5 days, or can be frozen for months in ice cube trays for baby servings or freezer-safe containers for larger servings.

sweet potatoes with butter, bone broth and sea salt

Sweet potatoes are one of my favorite sources of the slow-burning, dietary fiber type of energy to feed kids. Sweet potatoes are such a simple food, but they pack a really big vitamin and mineral punch in addition to a sustaining energy.

Since sweet potatoes are naturally very sweet, they will become a favorite finger food as baby enters toddlerhood, too!

Sweet potatoes, cubed

Splashes of water or bone broth
(see bone broth recipe on page 184)

Butter

Sea salt

steaming method

Steam the sweet potatoes in your steamer for 30 minutes and then blend to puree, adding splashes of water or bone broth to get the desired texture. You can use a food processor or blender.

pan-sauté method

Warm your pan over medium heat, add 2 to 3 tablespoons (25 to 38 g) of butter to melt per 2 cups (266 g) of sweet potato, and then add sweet potato with a few pinches of sea salt to soften and sweeten the sweet potatoes. You can cook more than 2 cups (266 g) at a time if you plan to freeze it for later use.

Cook the sweet potatoes over medium heat until they are softened, about 15 to 20 minutes. Pour the sweet potatoes into your blender or food processor, including the cooking fat left in the pan, and puree until smooth. Thin the puree out with water or bone broth to your baby's liking.

When serving baby, start with a tablespoon (15 ml) of sweet potato puree, and add a teaspoon of butter along with a pinch of sea salt and stir to combine. When baby starts finger foods, the cubed sweet potatoes can be put on the plate and fed finger-food style.

Leftovers from either method can be kept in the fridge for about 5 days, or can be frozen for months in ice cube trays for baby servings or freezer-safe containers.

cauliflower with butter and sea salt

Cooked cauliflower with butter is one of those matches made in heaven: smooth, creamy and flavorful. Baby is really going to like this one!

For its neutral white color, common cauliflower is surprisingly rich in vitamins C and K! The friendly fat in the butter will help the cauliflower to be digested easily and will help baby's digestive system absorb the fat-soluble vitamins.

Cauliflower florets, fresh or frozen

Splashes of water or bone broth (see bone broth recipe on page 184)

Butter

Sea salt

steaming method

Steam the cauliflower in your steamer for 25 minutes. If you are using frozen cauliflower, you don't even have to thaw it! Just dump it into the steamer right from the freezer. Blend to puree, adding splashes of water or bone broth to make the texture the way you want it. You can use a food processor or blender.

pan-sauté method

Warm your pan over medium heat, add 2 to 3 tablespoons (30 to 45 g) of butter to melt per 2 cups (200 g) of cauliflower, and then add the cauliflower with a few pinches of sea salt. If you are using frozen cauliflower, this method works best if the cauliflower is thawed first. You can cook more than 2 cups (200 g) at a time if you plan to freeze some for later use.

Cook the cauliflower over medium heat until it is softened, about 15 to 20 minutes. Pour the cauliflower into your blender or food processor, including the cooking fat left in the pan, and puree until smooth. Thin the puree with water or bone broth to your baby's liking.

When serving baby, start with a tablespoon (15 ml) of cauliflower puree, and add a teaspoon of butter along with a pinch of sea salt and stir to combine.

Leftovers from either method can be kept in the fridge for about 5 days, or can be frozen for months in ice cube trays for baby servings or freezer-safe containers for larger servings.

beets with beet greens, coconut oil, bone broth and sea salt

Creating a love for beets is a great goal when you are starting to feed your baby. Beets are not only loaded with essential vitamins and minerals for cell growth and function, but they naturally fight inflammation in the body as well as contain many anti-cancer compounds.

And don't forget those beet greens! They are easy to toss out or into the compost, but the beet greens in themselves are full of naturally occurring vitamin C, fiber and minerals and can be added to any pan of veggies to sauté or to any green smoothie. The recipe as written makes enough to feed three small children (including baby) and two adults, or makes 2 to 3 cups (475 to 710 ml) of puree just for baby, depending on how thick you make the puree.

3 tbsp (45 ml) coconut oil

3 medium beets, washed, peeled and cubed

Beet greens from the beets, chopped

Splashes of water or bone broth (see bone broth recipe on page 184)

Sea salt to taste

Warm a skillet over medium heat, melt the coconut oil in the skillet and toss in the beets. Add a pinch of sea salt to soften and sweeten the beets as they cook. Cook the beets for 7 to 10 minutes until they soften.

Add the beet greens and cook 3 minutes until the greens wilt.

Puree the cooked beets and greens with splashes of bone broth and sea salt to taste.

When serving baby, start with a tablespoon (15 ml) of beet puree. You can leave some of the beets as they are and serve them to the rest of the family. When baby gets to the finger-food age, you can serve the cooked cubed beets and wilted greens right on the plate.

Leftovers can be kept in the fridge for about 5 days, or can be frozen for months in ice cube trays for baby servings or freezer-safe containers for larger.

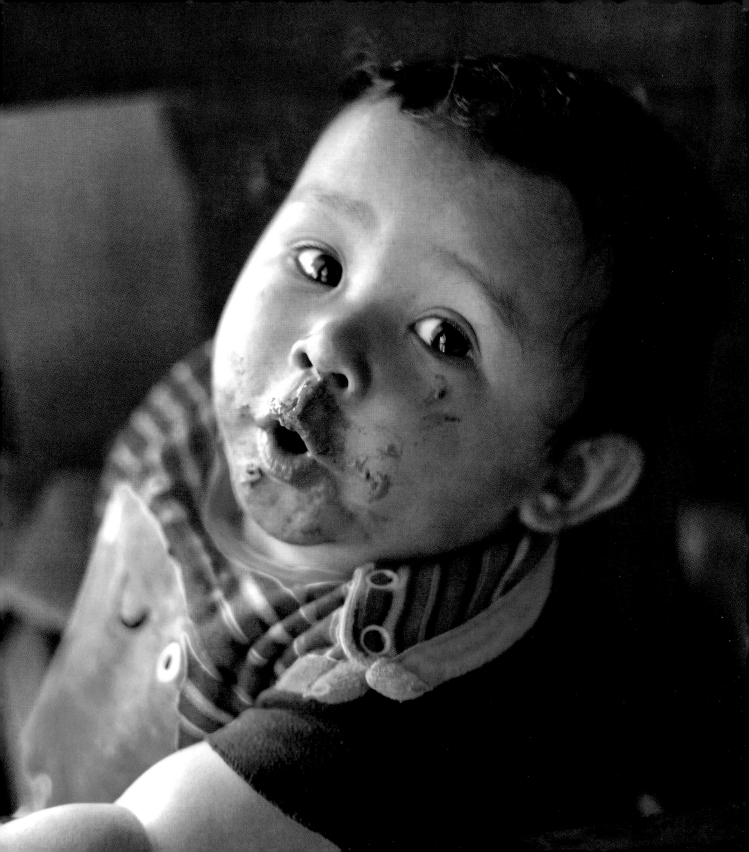

chapter 2

meat and fish purees

Many people shy away from from giving meat and fish to baby, thinking the flavor and texture will be too much. While baby doesn't have the teeth to chew these foods, for hundreds of years mothers used to pre-chew liver and meat for their babies, and these items were considered some of the most sacred and nutritionally important foods a baby could be eating, besides mother's milk. The nutritional profile of pastured and grass-fed animals as well as wild-caught fish is far superior to that of conventionally raised animals. It will benefit not only baby's growing brain and body, but will nourish the rest of the family as well. Developing a taste for wild-caught salmon and grass-fed beef will make for less dinner battles into the toddler years and will nourish baby with vitamin and mineral combinations essential for proper growth and development.

To find sources of grass-fed meat and pastured eggs as well as wild-caught fish, ask around at your farmers' markets and local Weston A. Price Foundation chapters, or search the Eat Wild website. I have found great sources of quality, well-raised animals just by striking up conversations at the farmers' markets in my area. Farmers love talking about their connections and sources!

soft-boiled pastured egg yolk with grated liver and sea salt

This meal is where it all began for my little ones. While this dish may not sound appetizing to an adult or a child who has never had it, these nutrient-rich egg yolks are creamy and delicious with a salty bite from the liver and sea salt. Egg yolks from pastured hens are rich in the cholesterol needed for brain development and have the same kind of omega-3 fatty acids found in mother's breast milk. Grated liver right from your freezer is easily added as an iron-rich component to the meal. This recipe makes one portion for baby.

1 pastured egg

Pinch of grated liver

Sea salt

soft-boil method in an electric steamer

Place the egg in your steamer and cook for 10 to 11 minutes. Every steamer releases steam a little differently, so you can start at 10 minutes and go from there. If your yolk comes out too hard, just add a splash of breast milk or water to it to mash it up.

Place the cooked egg into a bowl of cold water to stop the cooking and cool it so you can handle it.

soft-boil method in a pot of water

Fill a small or medium pot with water ¾ of the way up and bring to a boil. Using a slotted spoon, lower the egg into the boiling water and put the lid on the pot. Set your timer for 5 minutes. After 5 minutes, use a slotted spoon to take the egg out and place it in a bowl of cold water to stop the cooking and cool it so you can handle it.

After the egg is cool to the touch, crack the top, peel away the shell and white, and pour or scoop out the yolk into a small bowl or cup. Add a pinch of grated liver and sea salt, stir to combine and serve warm to baby.

notes: You can lightly sauté some liver in butter and freeze it in ice cube trays for quick and easy access for the egg prep. If you do not have access to a quality source of liver, simply omit this part or buy grass-fed desiccated liver capsules and pour that over the egg.

This meal does not freeze well. Time this feeding when you can be at home so you can serve it right away. You can keep any leftovers in the fridge for the same day, but after that the egg yolk should be used up. If I have anything left, I might stir it into another baby food puree to serve that day, add it to a smoothie for myself or scramble it into an egg for myself or another family member.

grass-fed beef roast with bone broth, marrow and sea salt

The aroma of a slow-cooked beef roast draws just about anyone to the kitchen ready to eat a delicious meal. Create a love for the best Sunday dinner right from the start! One 3- to 4-pound (1.4- to 1.8-kg) roast can feed a family of 5 with small children for 2 meals, so leftovers make a nice, quick weekday meal.

This juicy, tender grass-fed roast falls off the bone and is just so delicious. Grass-fed beef is superior to conventionally grown beef in so many ways. It is higher in beneficial omega-3 fats, cancer-fighting conjugated linoleic acid (CLA) and minerals such as calcium, magnesium and potassium. Compared to meat from feedlot animals, grass-fed beef is also higher in B vitamins. These elements are all crucial to baby's development, as well as to the health of the whole family.

---

1 medium onion, coarsely chopped

3 carrots, coarsely chopped

2 stalks of celery, coarsely chopped

3-4 lb (1.4-1.8 kg) grass-fed chuck roast

4 cloves of garlic, minced

Sea salt and pepper to taste

Bone broth and marrow for baby food prep (see page 184 for both the broth and marrow instructions)

slow-cooker method

Place the vegetables at the bottom of your slow cooker, and then put the beef roast on top. Fill the slow cooker with water half way up the roast, sprinkle the roast with the minced garlic, sea salt and pepper and cook on low for 8 hours.

slow-roasted oven method

Place the vegetables at the bottom of your roasting pan, and then put the beef roast on top. Fill the roasting pan with water half way up the roast, sprinkle the roast with the minced garlic, sea salt and pepper. Put the lid on and slow cook in the oven at 275°F (135°C) for 3 hours.

To prepare the beef for baby, puree the meat with marrow and bone broth to the desired consistency. Use however much marrow you have. I like to try for $\frac{1}{2}$ teaspoon or so per tablespoon (15 ml) of beef puree.

Leftovers from either method can be kept in the fridge for about 3 days, or can be frozen for months in ice cube trays for baby servings or freezer-safe containers for larger servings.

pastured turkey with sage-infused bone broth, butter and sea salt

Every November, our family farmer sells pasture-raised turkeys, and our family tradition of celebrating Thanksgiving is one that I have always wanted my kids to look forward to. When baby is ready to enjoy a special turkey dinner with the family, you can create a simple baby food–style meal with all of those amazing turkey dinner flavors!

Don't forget to save your turkey bones and carcass for bone broth. Turkey broth is hands-down my favorite bone broth. It is super rich and flavorful but not too overpowering. You can find the recipe for bone broth on page 184. The 12-pound (5.4-kg) turkey will make plenty of leftovers to use for a week or freeze. I find it feeds my family of 5 for 3 to 4 meals.

Note: This recipe will need to be planned in advance, allowing 2 to 3 days for the turkey to brine.

---

1 (12-lb [5.4-kg]) fresh turkey

4 tbsp (60 g) sea salt

1 tbsp (8 g) garlic powder

1 tbsp (3 g) dried thyme leaves

2 tsp (1.5 g) dried sage

¼ cup (60 g) butter

1 cup (240 ml) bone broth (see bone broth recipe on page 184)

1 sage leaf

Place the turkey, breast-side up, in a roasting pan fitted with a wire rack.

Whisk the sea salt, garlic powder, thyme and sage in a small bowl. This is your "dry brine."

Gently lift the skin on the breast of the turkey, and spread some of the dry brine onto the breasts using your hands. Spread more dry brine into the cavity of the turkey and then sprinkle the rest on the surface of the turkey (breast, legs, wings).

Cover the turkey with beeswax wrap, or plastic wrap if you don't have beeswax wrap, and place it in the refrigerator for 2 to 3 days. This gives the dry brine time to work on the meat to make it nice and tender and flavorful.

The night before you plan to cook the turkey, take off the wrap and place the turkey back in the refrigerator overnight to dry out completely. The dry skin will make for a nice crispy skin once it is cooked.

Take the turkey out of the fridge an hour before you plan to put it in the oven. This is so it can come to room temperature. Preheat the oven to 325°F (162°C).

Flip the turkey over to breast-side down and roast in the oven at 325°F (162°C) for 2 hours.

After 2 hours, turn the heat up to 425°F (218°C), flip the turkey breast-side up, brush with butter and roast for 30 minutes. Let the turkey rest about 30 minutes before carving.

To prepare the sage-infused bone broth for baby, simply put the bone broth and sage leaf in a saucepan and bring to a low simmer for about 10 minutes. Season the bone broth with sea salt to taste, and puree baby's turkey with splashes of the sage bone broth. Add about a ½ teaspoon of butter per tablespoon (15 ml) of turkey puree.

Once baby is at the finger-food age, you can shred bits of turkey to eat finger-food style. You can use the sage bone broth to dip the turkey in or drizzle it over top.

slow cooker pastured chicken with bone broth, butter and sea salt

Cooking a whole chicken every week or so quickly became my favorite easy meal of the week as my babies have grown into kids. For a long while, I have made my busiest day of the week chicken day at my house because I just don't have to think about it; it is a very simple supper!

This slow-cooker method makes mouth-watering, fall-off-the-bone meat, and fills your home with the smell of a warm, comforting dinner. Don't forget to save bones to make bone broth! This money-saving approach to using the whole bird will reward you weekly with nutrient-dense bone broth for baby and the whole family's meals. The recipe as written makes enough to feed three small children (including baby) and two adults for two dinners, or yields 5 cups (1.2 L) of puree just for baby, depending on how thick you make the puree.

1 medium onion, coarsely chopped

3 carrots, coarsely chopped

2 stalks of celery, coarsely chopped

4 cloves of garlic, minced

5–6 lbs (2.2-2.7 kg) pastured chicken

Sea salt and pepper to taste

Bone broth and butter for baby food prep (see bone broth recipe on page 184)

Place the vegetables and garlic at the bottom of your slow cooker, and then put the chicken on top of the vegetables, breast down.

Fill the slow cooker with water halfway up the chicken, sprinkle the chicken with sea salt and pepper and cook on low for 8 hours.

To prepare the chicken for baby, puree a tablespoon (15 ml) of meat with ½ teaspoon of bone broth and butter to the desired consistency for baby.

Leftovers can be kept in the fridge for about 3 days, or can be frozen for months in ice cube trays for baby servings or freezer-safe containers for larger servings.

note: The liquid left in the slow cooker is called meat stock. While not the same as bone broth, it is still very nutrient-dense and flavorful. I strain off this liquid and use it in soups and stews. It helps me stretch the bone broth that we go through so fast as a family of five!

wild-caught fish with bone broth and whole sour cream

If you live in an area where there is access to fresh, wild-caught fish, introducing baby to these brain-boosting fatty fish is a great idea. A simple pan-sear on a salmon takes less than 10 minutes and is a nice, quick meal for the whole family.

The creamy tang of sour cream is my favorite dip for salmon, and my babies always really took to this as well!

Wild-caught salmon fillets

Sea salt and pepper to taste

2 tbsp (28 g) butter

2 tbsp (30 ml) avocado oil (or pastured lard, or more butter is fine too)

Bone broth and sour cream for baby food prep

Sprinkle the fillets with sea salt and pepper on both sides while your skillet warms to medium-high heat with the butter and oil in it.

Add the seasoned salmon fillets to your hot skillet and let them cook until golden brown, about 4 to 5 minutes.

Flip the salmon over and cook another few minutes until the other side is golden brown. You can take it a little further on the heat if you like the skin really crispy.

To prepare for baby, puree the fish with a splash of bone broth. When serving, stir in ½ teaspoon of sour cream per 1 tablespoon (15 ml) of puree.

Leftovers can be kept in the fridge for about 3 days, or can be frozen for several months in ice cube trays for baby servings or freezer-safe containers for larger servings.

notes: To find sources of wild-caught fish, ask around at your farmers' markets and local Weston A. Price Foundation chapters, or search the Eat Wild website online. While I am surrounded by fresh-water lakes, the sourcing of fish where I live is not great, and it can be very expensive. One alternative that I have found helpful is to use wild-caught tuna and salmon in cans, such as the Wild Plant brand. This is a sustainable source, and many big-box as well as regular grocery stores carry them at very good prices. The fish is already prepared as well so it is as easy as blending up the meat with a little bone broth and you're done!

pastured liver pâté for baby

This nutrient-packed meal can be a quick snack for baby any time of the day, and it makes for a nice finger food for your toddlers with homemade bread, crackers or veggie sticks. Liver is a fantastic source of vital vitamin A, all of the B vitamins, iron and minerals that many of us are deficient in today such as copper and zinc. Both recipes on this page make 4 to 5 servings for three small children (including baby) and two adults, or about 8 to 10 baby-sized servings.

1 tbsp (14 g) butter

Sea salt to taste

½ medium onion, coarsely chopped

½ lb (230 g) raw chicken or beef liver, coarsely chopped

½ cup (120 ml) bone broth (see bone broth recipe on page 184)

1–2 tsp (1–2 g) dried thyme leaves, depending on your preference

Pepper to taste

Crackers, bread or veggie sticks for serving (optional)

Melt the butter in a pan and add the onion with a small pinch of sea salt to bring out the juices and sweeten them. Cook on medium heat for about 7 minutes until the onion is soft and sweet.

Add the liver, bone broth and thyme and bring to a low simmer for about 10 minutes. The liver will start to fall apart a little bit; this is okay! Pour the cooked liver with the liquid mixture into your food processor or blender and puree until smooth. Taste for salt and pepper and season accordingly.

Serve to baby on a spoon. Serve to the family with crackers, on sourdough bread or with veggie sticks. As baby gets older, he or she will have seen you dip your pâté and will want to start doing it too! Leftovers can be kept in the fridge for about 3 days, or can be frozen for months in ice cube trays for baby servings or in freezer-safe containers.

how to best cook organ meat for baby

Organ meats such as heart, liver and tongue are amazing superfood powerhouses. Because organ meat can be a little tough, as well as bland, I have always found it best to prepare it ground or grated and cooked alongside more palatable meat like beef. As baby approaches toddler age, these organ meat/beef combos make for great meatloaves, meatballs and patties for eating finger-food style.

½ lb (230 g) grass-fed ground beef

¼ lb (113 g) grass-fed organ meat such as heart, liver and/or tongue, either ground, finely chopped or grated if it is frozen

1 tsp sea salt

¼ tsp pepper

¼ cup (60 g) butter

In a small mixing bowl, combine the ground beef, organ meat, salt and pepper. Melt the butter in a skillet over medium-high heat and add the ground beef and organ meat mixture, and cook until everything is browned.

To serve baby, puree the beef and organ meat mixture with splashes of bone broth. You can also serve the bits of cooked ground meat finger-food style if baby is ready for that. The meat in ground or grated form and cooked this way makes it pretty easy to chew and handle.

chapter 3

fruit purees

Introducing a variety of fruit will provide baby with many beneficial vitamins and minerals, as well as delicious new flavors. While fruit is not necessarily a food to serve at every meal, it is important to train baby's palate to the variety of textures that fruit provides so that as babies become toddlers and school-aged children, a simple piece of fruit can be added to a meal or lunchbox as easy as can be!

You will notice that in each recipe the fruit is paired with a friendly fat for better vitamin absorption, as well as to help balance the sweetness in the fruit to keep blood sugars stable. When baby reaches finger-food age, a simple snack of blueberries and raw cheese will become a favorite!

I like to serve fruit purees at room temperature or right out of the fridge instead of warming them up. Older kids and adults usually eat fruit at room temperature, so I like to be sure my babies don't expect everything warmed up all the time. Once baby is picking up little pieces of finger food, you can cut up many of these fruits as on-the-go snacks!

avocado with banana

Avocados, which are known for their amazing friendly fat content, are also a fantastic food to start when baby is young. Getting baby excited about avocados will reward you with toddlers who will spoon avocado right out of the shell as a quick snack and eat fresh guacamole for a healthy taco night without a fuss. Bananas are a nice, gentle first fruit to start baby with because there is a natural amylase in the (ripe) banana which helps break down the carbohydrate.

This is as quick and simple as it gets, too! This recipe makes one portion for baby.

¼ ripe avocado

¼ ripe banana

Use the back of a fork to mash the avocado and banana together in a bowl and serve. You can puree in a food processor or blender if you wish. You might need to add a splash of breast milk or water to help it along as it blends.

notes: While this meal doesn't store in the freezer well because of browning, bananas and avocados come in their own travel packaging! You can pop a banana and avocado in your bag for a snack any time.

If baby doesn't finish all of this, you can store the leftovers in the fridge for the day and try it later. You can add it to a smoothie for yourself too! At the beginning, you can make a smaller portion, such as 1 tablespoon (15 ml) each of banana and avocado to mash.

When baby is ready to start playing with some finger foods on the table, you can chunk up some soft banana and avocado. These were some of my favorite first finger foods for my babies.

mashed raw mango with whole yogurt

Mango is another great first fruit for baby because of its mild sweetness. It is rich in prebiotic fiber as well as many vitamins and minerals. Babies digest mango well without the need for cooking, so it is a great on-the-go snack and is easily cubed for finger food.

Since I like to serve fruit with a satiating friendly fat, probiotic rich whole yogurt is a nice choice for mango. As baby gets older, cubed mango in a little cup of whole plain yogurt makes a great afternoon snack or breakfast addition.

Ripe mango pieces

Whole plain yogurt

Mash the mango flesh with the back of your fork, or if you prefer, you can puree it in a food processor or blender with a splash of breast milk or water.

To serve to baby, stir in 1 teaspoon whole plain yogurt per 1 tablespoon (15 ml) of mashed mango.

Leftovers can be kept in the fridge for about 5 days, or can be frozen for months in ice cube trays for baby servings or freezer-safe containers for larger servings.

note: Frozen mango works fine if fresh, ripe mangoes are not available. Just be sure there is no added sugar or other preservatives in the ingredient list.

mashed raw papaya with whole sour cream

Papaya is another mildly sweet fruit that makes a nice introduction to fruit but will not overwhelm baby's palate.

Papaya is very rich in vitamin C and many minerals. Since papaya is easy to digest, it does not need to be cooked and is a very easy prep for baby. I like to tame the sweet with a little tangy sour cream, which also adds some probiotic benefit to the meal.

Papaya, de-seeded and scooped out of the shell

Whole sour cream

Mash the papaya flesh with the back of your fork, or if you prefer, you can puree it in a food processor or blender with a splash of breast milk or water.

To serve to baby, stir in 1 teaspoon whole sour cream per 1 tablespoon (15 ml) of mashed papaya.

Leftovers can be kept in the fridge for about 5 days, or can be frozen for months in ice cube trays for baby servings or freezer-safe containers for larger servings.

note: Frozen papaya works fine if fresh, ripe papaya is not available. Just be sure there is no added sugar or other preservatives in the ingredient list.

steamed apples with coconut butter

Fresh applesauce is a family favorite in my house, as we live in an area with an abundance of apples in the fall! Cooked apples fill your home with the smell of fall and apple pie.

Since fruit like apples have more pectin which can be hard on developing digestive systems, it is important not to just give baby fresh apples that have been blended. Cooking the apples breaks down the pectin and makes the apples easier to digest. Creamy coconut butter tastes amazing with these apples and balances the carbohydrates with nourishing friendly fats.

Apples, cored and coarsely sliced

Coconut butter (see recipe on page 189)

Place the apples in your steamer and cook for 25 minutes.

Puree the apples in a food processor or blender until they are the desired consistency.

To serve baby, stir in 1 teaspoon coconut butter per 1 tablespoon (15 ml) of apple puree.

Leftovers can be kept in the fridge for about 5 days, or can be frozen for months in ice cube trays for baby servings or freezer-safe containers for larger servings.

note: If you don't have a steamer, you can bake your apples in a roasting pan. It makes the house smell so good! Add an inch (2.5 cm) or so of water to the bottom of your roasting pan, put the apple slices in and bake at 350°F (175°C) for 45 minutes. You can puree from there.

steamed pears with cinnamon and butter

The whole family is going to be begging for this recipe! Cooking sweet, juicy pears with warm cinnamon and creamy butter creates an intoxicating smell.

Pears are another fruit with a lot of pectin, so even if those pears are super soft and juicy, it is important to cook them before serving to break down that pectin for babies with developing digestive systems. The friendly fat in the butter will help balance the carbohydrates in the fruit as well.

Pears, cored and coarsely sliced

Cinnamon to taste (a little goes a long way, especially with babies)

Butter

Place the pear slices in the steamer and cook for 25 minutes.

Puree your cooked pears in a food processor or blender until they reach the desired consistency. Add the cinnamon to taste and blend to combine, or sprinkle the cinnamon as desired for each serving.

To serve baby, stir in 1 teaspoon butter per 1 tablespoon (15 ml) of pear puree.

Leftovers can be kept in the fridge for about 5 days, or can be frozen for months in ice cube trays for baby servings or freezer-safe containers for larger servings.

note: If you don't have a steamer, you can bake your pears in a roasting pan. Add an inch (2.5 cm) of water to the bottom of your roasting pan, put the pear slices in and bake at 350°F (175°C) for 45 minutes. Then you can puree from there.

steamed berries with coconut butter

Fresh berries will quickly become your toddler's favorite finger food and your school-aged children's favorite lunchbox addition, but before we get there, we can introduce baby to these sweet and tart flavors and bright, fun colors!

Blueberries, raspberries, strawberries and even small stone fruits like cherries and apricots need to be cooked for baby, to reduce the pectin for their developing digestive systems. I like to stir in some creamy coconut butter not only because the flavor is amazing, but also because the friendly fats help balance those fruit carbohydrates.

Berries of choice

Coconut butter (see coconut butter recipe on page 189)

Steam your berries for 20 minutes and then puree.

To serve to baby, stir in 1 teaspoon of coconut butter per 1 tablespoon (15 ml) of berry puree.

Leftovers can be kept in the fridge for about 5 days, or can be frozen for months in ice cube trays for baby servings or freezer-safe containers for larger servings.

*See photo on page 42.

notes: I like to keep some of the seedy texture in the berry puree. Some kids make faces at this texture and that is okay! Get their palates used to textures that are not super smooth. You will be glad you did because you will have toddlers who won't turn down a raspberry or a strawberry just because it has seeds.

If you don't have a steamer, you can sauté the berries on the stovetop. Just cover the bottom of your pan with water, place the berries in the pan, put the lid on and simmer them on low for about 15 minutes. You can puree them at this point.

sautéed peaches and cream

At the end of every summer, we visit the sweetest family. They grow a variety of stone fruits, from cherries to peaches, and we get to bring home the most delicious "right off the tree" fruit. A simple bowl of sliced peaches and fresh raw cream is one of our favorite summertime dishes. When I had really little ones around, giving those peaches a quick sauté softened them up enough for baby to manage. The cooking also breaks down the pectin in the fruit, making it easier for developing digestive systems to handle.

2 tbsp (60 g) butter

3 medium peaches, pitted and cubed

¼ cup (60 ml) raw cream

Warm a skillet over medium heat, melt the butter and add the peaches. Cook over medium heat for about 5 minutes until the peaches soften.

Take the peaches off the heat and stir in the cream. To prepare for baby, puree the peaches and cream mixture and serve 1 tablespoon (15 ml) at a time. You can serve the peaches finger-food style if baby is ready for that.

note: Yogurt, sour cream, coconut milk or coconut cream would work in place of the raw cream if you don't have that available. (See the recipe for homemade coconut milk on page 62.)

baby's first smoothie

Introduce baby to his or her first smoothie using two very simple but nourishing ingredients. Milk kefir is a delicious fermented milk. It is easy on digestion and nourishing to gut flora as well as filled with minerals to nourish development. This quick-prep smoothie is a great way to introduce a straw because it tastes so good! Once babies get a little taste of that smoothie, they quickly figure out how to get it back up that straw for more! This recipe makes 2 to 3 baby-sized servings, or 1 to 2 child-sized servings.

1 cup (240 ml) whole milk kefir

1 small to medium ripe banana

Blend the kefir and banana in a blender and serve. You can offer a straw, but if baby isn't catching on to the straw, you can use a spoon.

notes: You can purchase milk kefir grains to make your own kefir (for example through CulturesforHealth.com). Kefir is so easy to make and requires very little hands-on time. The directions for using the kefir grains come right with the package from Cultures for Health. You can also ask around at your local farmers' markets for anyone wanting to share their kefir grains that need splitting from growing.

chapter 4

drinks

These nutrient-dense drinks are great for the whole family to enjoy and are designed for babies to start taking sips around 6 months. These drinks should not replace breastfeeding or homemade formula, but pave the way to a broad taste palate through nourishing teas, broths, milks, etc. By starting sips of these nourishing drinks while babies are young, you will be rewarded with toddlers who gladly drink a teacup of bone broth with their lunch, or who will sip on a healing herbal tea when they are ill.

I used a medicine syringe to feed drinks like buttered bone broth and tea to my very small babies, around 5 to 7 months. It works well and is less messy than a small spoon. While I don't mind the use of sippy cups here and there, especially for travel, I find straws and open cups work well for babies, too. My second two babies transitioned to using open cups so much better than my first whom I kept on sippy cups far too long. When first introducing these drinks, I just gave baby sips from my mug or used the medicine syringe. I invested in some small teacups that I love using for warm drinks for my older babies as well. While every baby learns how to do things at a different pace, I did find that my babies took to them well. They use a straw for a while and then by 18 months learn how to drink from the open cup.

buttered bone broth

This was the first drink other than breast milk that I served to my babies, right around 5 to 6 months. Just a few sips here and there from my mug created older babies and toddlers who easily down a teacup of buttered broth for a mid-morning snack, or as a healing, hydrating drink when they are ill. Bone broth is a gentle mineral source for baby, and the added butter fat helps absorption of vitamins as well as digestion.

The butter creates a creamy, frothy top when blended and is a great afternoon pick-me-up for momma!

yield: 1 child-sized serving

½ cup (120 ml) bone broth
(see bone broth recipe on page 184)

½ tsp butter

Pinch of sea salt to taste

Warm the bone broth over the stove and stir in the butter and sea salt to taste. You can use an immersion blender, regular blender or single-serve-drink type blender (such as Magic Bullet) to blend and create a frothy top if you wish. It's not necessary but I enjoy it this way!

note: Keep in mind that my recipe for bone broth (page 184) is rarely salted so I have to add a decent pinch of sea salt for this drink. If you salt your bone broth, you may not need to add additional salt.

nutrient-dense raw milk or kefir tonic

A favorite bedtime snack for my toddlers, this raw milk tonic is a nice satiating drink to nourish a rapidly growing body and developing brain in little ones. It is rich and creamy with a hint of warming molasses that also provides a great mineral-boosting punch for baby.

yield: 1 child-sized serving

½ cup (120 ml) raw milk or kefir

1 tsp raw cream

1 raw pastured egg yolk

½ to 1 tsp blackstrap molasses

cold version

Blend everything with an immersion blender, in a regular blender or in a single-serve-drink blender until combined well and then serve to baby.

warm version

Gently warm the raw milk but only until it is warm to the touch. Don't overheat.

Add the rest of the ingredients and blend with an immersion blender. Or pour the warm milk into a blender with the rest of the ingredients to blend, and then serve to baby.

For younger babies around 6 to 7 months, feeding this to baby on a spoon works well. A straw works wonderfully and when baby is ready to use one, you can serve this like a smoothie. I like to use small mason jelly jars.

notes: Leftovers can be stored in the fridge for 24 hours. If you need to use them up, leftovers are great added to a smoothie!

It is important to use yolks from hens that have been on pasture from a trusted source if you plan to use the raw yolk. If you do not have a good source, or if you don't feel comfortable using raw yolks, simply omit this ingredient. You could use a teaspoon of avocado oil or olive oil for fat, or more cream.

how to make coconut milk

Coconut milk is rich and creamy and not only is delicious to drink on its own, but also makes a great dairy-free milk to use in recipes if the family happens to be dairy-free.

While my family has always tolerated raw dairy just fine, I tended to get my babies used to coconut milk as well. It is nice to change things up once in a while, and coconut milk is rich in healthy fats. Unfortunately, store-bought coconut milk has additives and gums that can be irritating to baby's tummy, so homemade is preferable as well as easy!

yield: 1 ½ quarts (1.5 L)

7 cups (530 g) unsweetened coconut shreds

7 cups (1680 ml) water, brought to a boil

Put the coconut in a large mixing bowl, and pour the boiling water over the coconut shreds.

Cover the bowl with a towel and let the coconut steep 2 to 3 hours.

Pour the water and coconut-shred mixture into a blender and blend about a minute. Pour the blended coconut and water mixture into a cheesecloth or tea towel over a bowl and squeeze out the milk.

Coconut milk is great to drink on its own, but it also works well in smoothies. I like to use a straw to feed it to my younger ones. You can use a medicine syringe for really little ones. If you plan on coconut milk being your main milk source in the house, it is nice to get baby used to the taste around 6 months. Again, this isn't replacing breast milk or homemade formula, rather just getting baby used to the flavor and feel of it.

note: Store the milk in the fridge for a week or in the freezer for 6 months. Shake the coconut milk before serving; the cream will separate.

nutrient-dense coconut milk tonic

Rich and creamy with mild coconut sweetness, this coconut milk tonic will nourish baby with friendly fats and mineral-rich egg yolk and warm molasses. Coconut is rich in lauric acid, almost identical to the lauric acid found in breast milk and helps to protect the immune system. This is a very nourishing drink and also makes for a great snack for toddlers.

yield: 1 child-sized serving

½ cup (120 ml) coconut milk
(see coconut milk recipe on page 62)

1 raw pastured egg yolk

½–1 tsp blackstrap molasses

cold version

Blend everything with an immersion blender, in a regular blender or in a single-serving blender until the mixture is combined well and ready to serve to baby.

warm version

Gently warm the coconut milk, but only until it is warm to the touch. Don't overheat.

Add the rest of the ingredients and blend with an immersion blender. Or pour the warm milk into a blender with the rest of the ingredients to blend, and then serve to baby.

For younger babies around 6 to 7 months, it works well to feed this to them with a spoon. When babies are ready to use a straw, it works well to serve this like a smoothie. I like to use small Mason or jelly jars.

Leftovers can be stored in the fridge for 24 hours and are great added into a smoothie.

simple nettle tea for baby

Mineral-rich nettles are an immune-boosting and mineral-balancing herbal powerhouse! Getting baby used to these bitter herbs will reward you with toddlers and school-aged children who will gladly drink nettle tea. It makes a nourishing drink while children are ill and I like to pack it in lunches for my school-aged children to give them a mineral boost during a long day of school.

yield: 1 child-sized serving

2 tsp (2 g) loose nettle leaves

½ cup (120 ml) hot water

Drizzle of blackstrap molasses for babies under age 1 or raw honey for babies over age 1 (optional)

Steep the nettles in the hot water for 5 minutes and strain.

Stir in the molasses or raw honey, if desired, and serve to baby. You can use a medicine syringe to serve if baby hasn't caught on to using a straw yet. Sippy cups work fine as well.

notes: The recipe makes enough for 1 child-sized serving, but baby may have only a few tablespoons before feeling full or being done.

Stinging nettles grow as abundant "weeds" in our backyard woods, so I harvest and dry our own and my supply lasts through the year. If you are harvesting fresh nettles, be sure to wear gloves and only harvest from a clean, pollution-free source. Otherwise, you can find dry nettles at your local health food store or you can order them online. I tend to make larger batches of tea for everyone to drink at the same time. The general rule of thumb for making tea or infusions is 1 tablespoon (3 g) of herbs per 1 cup (240 ml) of hot water.

nettle and hibiscus infusion

This delicious infusion made its way to my house on a daily basis when I was recovering after the birth of my third baby. I was drinking nettle infusions daily for mineral balancing, and one day my 2-year-old just started guzzling down my cup of nettle and hibiscus infusion! She loved it!

Infusions are a bit stronger than teas as they steep longer and are more concentrated. The addition of the slightly sweet and tart hibiscus cuts through the bitter nettles during the infusion, making a delicious and colorful mineral-rich drink for the whole family! Since I knew we could all use a mineral boost, I started making 2 quarts (2 L) of this infusion almost every day for us to share as a family.

yield: 1 quart (1 L)

---

3 tsp (3 g) loose-leaf nettles herb

1–2 tsp (1–2 g) hibiscus herb

1 quart (1 L) hot water

Drizzle of blackstrap molasses for babies under age 1 or raw honey for babies over age 1 (optional)

Steep the nettles and hibiscus in the hot water for up to 8 hours and strain.

Stir in the molasses or raw honey, if desired, and serve. You can use a medicine syringe for serving if baby hasn't caught on to using a straw yet. Sippy cups work fine as well.

notes: This recipe makes enough for several child-sized servings ($\frac{1}{2}$ cup to 1 cup [118 ml to 237 ml]) or one adult serving.

I like to put the juice of half a lemon in my infusion and my older girls enjoy that too. Avoid feeding citrus fruits to babies until they are older than one year because the acid can be bothersome to tiny tummies.

electrolyte rehydrating drink

It is inevitable that at some point our kids will come down with a cold of some sort! Even the healthiest children will eventually have to fight off a bug; while they rest and recover, it is important to keep them hydrated and flush the bug out of their system.

Mineral-rich bone broth is always my first option for hydrating sick children. Sometimes, though, they just need something different to drink, and this simple rehydrating drink is safer than the commercial rehydrating drinks at the store.

yield: 1 pint (475 ml)

2 cups (475 ml) water

2-4 tbsp (30-60 ml) mango or papaya puree

$\frac{1}{8}$ tsp sea salt, Celtic salt or Himalayan salt

2 tsp (10 ml) blackstrap molasses

Place everything into a pint (475-ml) jar, put the lid on and shake vigorously until the mixture is combined, then serve.

Leftovers can be refrigerated up to 3 days. I like to keep the pint jar in the fridge and just pour a little into a small teacup or sippy cup for drinking. This recipe is perfect for the whole family, so you can double this into a quart (1-L) jar to share with everyone!

notes: This recipe makes enough for several child-sized servings ($\frac{1}{2}$ cup to 1 cup [118 ml to 237 ml]) or one adult serving.

Please note that babies who are still nursing ought to be nursing exclusively during illness. Supplementing bone broth if they are willing is fine, but if I still have a nursing baby, my number one go-to in hydration is breast milk. If baby's hydration is of concern and is not improving, seek medical attention.

If baby is over age 1, raw honey may be used in place of the molasses, and the juice of half a lemon may be used in place of the mango or papaya puree.

tummy-calming fennel tea for baby

Fennel is a very gentle digestive aid for tiny tummies and can help relax the intestines. It is also known as a very mild laxative and can help with occasional constipation in baby.

Fennel has a mild licorice flavor that some little ones take right to and others do not. I like to add a drizzle of blackstrap molasses, or raw honey if baby is over the age of 1 year, if baby isn't quite into it at first.

yield: 1 child-sized serving

½ cup (120 ml) hot water

½ tsp fennel seeds

Drizzle of blackstrap molasses or raw honey (optional)

Steep the fennel seeds in hot water for 30 minutes and strain.

You can drizzle in some molasses or honey if you wish, and serve. Use a medicine syringe to serve if baby hasn't caught on to using a straw yet. Sippy cups work fine as well.

notes: The recipe makes enough for 1 child-sized serving, but baby may have only a few tablespoons before feeling full or being done.

If you are nursing, you can drink this tea yourself and pass the benefits along to baby.

If baby is having continued digestive distress or symptoms worsen, please seek medical attention.

colic-calming chamomile and lemon balm tea for baby

This is a nice tea for baby to get used to; not only does it safely and naturally help calm a fussy baby, it can also help older children who may have a hard time winding down for bed or may not be feeling well from illness and can't fall asleep.

The mild, sweet lemon flavor is very pleasant to young palates and is very comforting with a splash of raw cream or coconut milk.

yield: 1 child-sized serving

½ tsp loose-leaf chamomile

¼ tsp loose-leaf lemon balm

½ cup (120 ml) hot water

1 tsp raw cream or coconut milk
(see coconut milk recipe on page 62)

Steep the chamomile and lemon balm in the hot water for 10 minutes and strain.

Stir in the raw cream or coconut milk and serve. You can use a medicine syringe to serve if baby hasn't caught on to using a straw yet. Sippy cups work fine as well.

notes: The recipe makes enough for 1 child-sized serving, but baby may have only a few tablespoons before feeling full or being done.

This tea is great for the whole family. If there are leftovers, you can just drink it yourself! If you are nursing, you can drink this tea and pass the benefits along to baby. I liked to drink chamomile tea around dinnertime so it was within an hour or two of baby's bedtime.

fever-aiding yarrow and lemon balm tea for baby

Having sick little ones is never any fun. Our bodies are pretty amazing at fighting off illness, and if your goal is to avoid fever-reducing medicines from the store while achieving the same effect, this yarrow tea is just for you!

While letting that fever do its job of fighting the infection, it can really make our kids uncomfortable. Yarrow does a great job of naturally bringing a higher fever down. Lemon balm brings a mild, sweet lemon flavor, and can help relax those fever aches and help babies sleep.

yield: 1 child-sized serving

½ tsp loose-leaf yarrow

¼ tsp loose-leaf lemon balm

½ cup (120 ml) hot water

Drizzle of blackstrap molasses for babies under age 1 or raw honey for babies over age 1 (optional)

Steep the yarrow and lemon balm in the hot water for 10 minutes and strain.

You can stir in a drizzle of molasses or raw honey if you wish. Serve. Use a medicine syringe to serve if baby hasn't caught on to using a straw yet. Sippy cups work fine as well.

notes: The recipe makes enough for 1 child-sized serving, but baby may have only a few tablespoons before feeling full or being done.

If you are nursing, you can drink this tea yourself and pass the benefits along to baby.

You can make a larger batch and steep it longer for a stronger tea to add to a bath. These herbal tea baths can help with a higher fever and relax babies.

If baby's fever is persistent, and baby is lethargic and/or symptoms worsen, please seek medical attention.

chapter 5

simple soup starts for babies, toddlers and the whole family

These are delicious and simple soups for babies, toddlers and the whole family to enjoy! You will hardly notice that these soups are loaded with vegetables because the flavors are so amazing. These make great lunches or sides to dinner and are a great way to start transitioning off of baby food purees. Once you have determined that baby is tolerating single-vegetable purees, getting those vegetables combined with other flavors in these delicious soups is the next step toward full meals. These simple soups will even go beyond those babyhood years to make great lunches for toddlers and big-kid thermos additions to the lunchbox.

I also invite you to put your signature on these simple soups! Try dressing them up with your own favorite seasonings, those your family is used to or those eaten locally where you live. Make these soups as thin or thick and creamy as you want. Try a straw for toddlers who are wanting to "do it myself" and aren't quite getting the soup to their mouths before it makes a mess! I also like to start trying that straw out around 6 to 9 months to get them used to using one.

creamy roasted carrot soup

Roasting carrots and onions does some sort of magic, making them lightly sweet but also rich and full. This creamy carrot soup is not only loaded with the antioxidants, minerals and vitamins found in carrots and gelatin-rich bone broth, but is also a good helping of whole, nourishing fats from yogurt to make this a satisfying and balanced light meal.

yield: 4 quarts (4 L)

---

2 lbs (900 g) organic carrots, quartered coarsely

2 medium onions, peeled, halved and each half quartered

4 cloves garlic, kept in the skin

$\frac{1}{3}$ cup (75 g) butter, melted

$2\frac{1}{2}$ tsp (12.5 g) sea salt

2 quarts (2 L) bone broth (see bone broth recipe on page 184)

2 tsp (1 g) minced fresh basil or 1 tsp dry basil

$1\frac{1}{2}$ cups (360 ml) whole yogurt or sour cream

Sea salt and pepper to taste

Divide the carrots, onions and garlic between two sheet pans and toss with the butter and sea salt until everything is evenly coated.

Roast at 450°F (230°C) for 40 to 45 minutes until everything is caramelized and soft.

Slide the roasted carrots and onions into your soup pot, and squeeze the garlic from its skin into the pot as well. Add the bone broth and basil and bring to a low simmer for 7 minutes.

Add the yogurt and puree the soup with an immersion blender right in the pot, or transfer to a blender to puree. Season with sea salt and pepper to taste. Serve baby about a tablespoon (15 ml) or so of soup right from the spoon to start with. You can use a straw for older babies and toddlers if that works better for them.

You can store leftovers in the fridge for 5 to 7 days, or in the freezer for months.

note: Just a tip on the roasted garlic so you don't burn your fingers! I like to pull them off the baking sheet onto my cool counter while I slide everything else off into the pan and get my broth going. In just those few minutes, the roasted garlic will cool off enough to allow you to squeeze it out of its peel.

pea soup

This is one of the very first soups I ever introduced my girls to, and I have been making it for years. It is always a family favorite for lunch, and it gets slurped down to the very last drop every time! Peas give a sweetness to the soup that is very kid-friendly.

Soup purees like pea soup are a great way to get mineral- and gelatin-rich bone broth into the whole family on a daily basis. And the great news is, the whole family can eat this soup together: no alterations, changes or extra food prep.

I love this recipe because there is seriously no fuss. Since the soup gets pureed in the end, there is no fancy dicing or slicing! It makes a great last-minute lunch or dinner, and the leftovers warm through quickly the next day, or can easily be packed up for work, school or day care.

yield: about 5 quarts (5 L)

3 tbsp (43 g) friendly fat to cook in, such as butter, coconut oil, tallow or lard

2-3 small to medium onions, sliced

Sea salt to taste

3-4 cloves garlic, coarsely chopped

1 (5-lb [2.2-kg]) bag organic frozen peas

1–1½ quarts (1–1.5 L) bone broth (see bone broth recipe on page 184)

Pepper to taste

Sour cream or cream to stir in or garnish (optional)

Warm your stockpot over medium to high heat, melt the friendly fat and add your onions to the pot to cook for about 7 minutes. Add a big pinch of salt while they cook to bring the juices out and let them sweeten up while they cook.

Add the garlic and cook a minute, and then add the peas and stock and bring to a boil.

Reduce to a simmer until the peas are cooked through—usually about 10 to 15 minutes.

Puree the soup with a blender or an immersion blender, and then add sea salt and pepper to taste.

Before serving the soup, put a dollop of sour cream on top if you'd like! Serve baby about a tablespoon (15 ml) or so of soup right from the spoon to start off with. You can use a straw for older babies and toddlers if that works better for them.

notes: I buy my peas in bulk at a big-box store (such as Costco). If your peas come in 1-pound (450-g) bags, you can either get 5 bags, or you can half this recipe and 2 bags should work fine.

You can store leftovers in the fridge for 5 to 7 days, or in the freezer for months. It is so nice to put half of the soup into the freezer to pull out on a busy day when you don't have time to cook!

squash medley soup

The delicious flavor profile of three beautiful winter squashes all in one bowl! This squash medley soup is savory and sweet, creamy and satisfying. It makes an almost weekly appearance in our bowls and my school-aged children's school thermoses during the fall and winter!

It is a great soup for the whole family, and because squash in particular is very gentle on digestion, it makes a great soup for baby's developing tummy.

yield: 5-6 quarts (5-6 L)

1 small acorn squash

1 small pie or sugar pumpkin

1 small butternut squash

¼ cup (60 ml) friendly fat to cook in, such as butter, lard, tallow, avocado oil or coconut oil

2 medium onions, sliced

Sea salt to taste

3 cloves garlic, coarsely chopped

3 quarts (3 L) bone broth, plus more depending on how thick you like your soup (see bone broth recipe on page 184)

2 tsp (10 ml) blackstrap molasses

Pepper to taste

Place all 3 squashes (whole) on a large baking sheet and roast in an oven at 425°F (220°C) for 1 hour and 15 minutes. When the squash are cool enough to handle, cut each in half and let them continue to cool while you start the rest of the soup.

Melt the friendly fat in the bottom of a large soup pot and add the onion with a pinch of sea salt to bring out the onion's juices and sweeten it. Cook on medium for 7 minutes.

Add the garlic and cook for a minute.

Scoop the seeds out of the squashes and discard. Scoop the squash out of their shells and add to the cooked onion and garlic along with the bone broth.

Bring the soup to a low simmer for about 5 minutes, turn the heat off and puree the soup with an immersion blender right in the pot, or in a regular blender. At this point you can add more bone broth or water if you want a thinner consistency.

Stir in the molasses and add sea salt and pepper to your taste. Serve baby about a tablespoon (15 ml) or so of soup right off the spoon to start with. You can use a straw for older babies and toddlers if that works better for them.

notes: You can use more of one type of squash if all three types aren't available.

You can store leftovers in the fridge for 5 to 7 days, or in the freezer for months. It is so nice to put half of the soup into the freezer to pull out on a busy day when you don't have time to cook!

simple broccoli soup

This creamy, rich broccoli soup has all of the flavor and texture of your favorite sandwich shop soup without the flour! The blended potatoes in the soup give a really smooth creamy texture. You will be glad that this soup stores so nicely in the freezer so you can pull it out easily for lunch every week!

yield: 7 quarts (7 L)

⅓ cup (75 g) friendly fat to cook in, such as butter, lard, tallow, avocado oil or coconut oil

4 lbs (1.8 kg) organic broccoli, either 1 (4-lb [1.8-kg]) frozen bag (thawed) or about 4 bunches broccoli, coarsely chopped, including the stalks

4 small onions, sliced

4 large carrots, coarsely chopped

3 medium to large potatoes, cubed

Sea salt to taste

7 cloves garlic, chopped

4 quarts (4 L) bone broth
(see bone broth recipe on page 184)

Pepper to taste

Whole raw cream or sour cream, to garnish in each bowl (optional)

In a large stockpot, melt the friendly fat and cook the broccoli, onion, carrot and potatoes with a few pinches of salt over medium heat for about 10 to 15 minutes, until the onions are clear and the broccoli is bright green.

Add the garlic and cook for a minute.

Add the bone broth and bring to a boil, then reduce to a simmer until the broccoli and carrots are soft and cooked through, about 15 minutes.

Turn the heat off, and puree the soup completely with an immersion blender or in a regular blender.

Add sea salt and pepper to taste. You can garnish each bowl of soup with a splash of whole raw cream to stir in or a dollop of sour cream. Serve baby about a tablespoon (15 ml) or so of soup right off the spoon to start with. You can use a straw for older babies and toddlers if that works better for them.

You can store leftovers in the fridge for 5 to 7 days, or in the freezer for months.

note: I buy my broccoli in bulk at a big-box store (Costco, for example). If your broccoli comes in 1-pound (450-g) bags, you can either get 4 bags, or you can half this recipe and 2 bags should work fine.

summer squash soup

When your farmers' markets or summer gardens are overflowing with zucchini and yellow squash, this is the recipe for you! Taking advantage of those in-season prices will afford you an abundance of this nourishing soup to put away in the freezer for later in the fall when you want a little taste of summer!

The soup seems simple, but the flavor is delicious and the texture creamy. Summer squashes, in particular, are loaded with natural minerals for balancing our bodies, so this makes a great meal for the whole family.

yield: 2½ quarts (2.5 L)

¼ cup (57 g) friendly fat to cook in, such as butter, tallow, lard, coconut oil or avocado oil

2 small to medium onions, coarsely chopped

2 medium carrots, coarsely chopped

2 celery stalks, coarsely chopped

3 medium zucchini, coarsely chopped

3 medium yellow summer squash, coarsely chopped

5-6 large cloves of garlic, minced

Sea salt to taste

1½ quarts (1.5 L) bone broth (see bone broth recipe on page 184)

⅛-¼ tsp cayenne (optional)

Pepper to taste

Whole sour cream and chives to garnish (optional)

Melt the butter or other fat in a soup pot and add the onion, carrot, celery, zucchini and yellow squash, along with a big pinch of sea salt to draw out the veggies' juices to sweeten them. Cook on medium heat for 10 to 15 minutes, stirring occasionally.

Add the garlic and cook for a minute.

Add the broth and cayenne and bring to a simmer for about 5 minutes.

Blend the soup with an immersion blender or in a regular blender, and season with sea salt and pepper to taste.

Garnish with a dollop of whole sour cream and chopped chives if you wish. Serve baby about a tablespoon (15 ml) or so of soup right off the spoon to start with. You can use a straw for older babies and toddlers if that works better for them.

You can store leftovers in the fridge for 5 to 7 days, or in the freezer for months.

hearty roasted root veggie soup

Roast a colorful array of root vegetables for this beautiful, sweet and creamy soup puree that the whole family will love to have with their lunch or dinner.

Taking advantage of those root veggies that grow in nutrient-rich soil, this soup is more than just comforting; it is packed with vitamins and minerals! When produce is slim during the winter months, this soup is a staple in our house.

yield: 6 quarts (6 L)

2 medium onions, peeled and quartered

2 medium sweet potatoes, cubed

2 medium yellow potatoes, cubed

1 medium to large turnip, cubed

2 large parsnips, coarsely chopped

6 large carrots, coarsely chopped

6 cloves garlic, with peels left on for roasting

½ cup (120 ml) melted butter for roasting

1 tbsp (15 g) sea salt, plus more to taste

2 tsp (4 g) pepper, plus more to taste

4 quarts (4 L) bone broth
(see bone broth recipe on page 184)

Put all of the cut veggies on 2 large sheet trays and toss with the butter, sea salt and pepper to coat evenly.

Roast the veggies at 425°F (220°C) for 20 minutes, rotate the trays in the oven, and roast another 20 to 25 minutes until the vegetables are caramelized and soft.

Transfer the roasted vegetables to a large soup or stockpot, squeeze the garlic out of its peel into the pot and add the bone broth. Bring the soup to a simmer for 5 minutes.

Puree the soup with an immersion blender right in the pot or transfer it to a regular blender to puree, and season with additional sea salt and pepper to taste.

Serve baby about a tablespoon (15 ml) or so of soup right off the spoon to start with. You can use a straw for older babies and toddlers if that works better for them.

You can store leftovers in the fridge for 5 to 7 days, or in the freezer for months.

notes: Let the garlic cool before attempting to squeeze it out of its paper covering. To prevent burning my fingers, I like to take the garlic off the tray and put it on the counter after roasting so it can cool while I get the rest of the veggies into the pot and get the bone broth going.

Sometimes I use 3 quarts (3 L) of broth and a quart (1 L) of water to stretch my broth since this is a big recipe; you can even use half water and half broth if you don't have that much broth around.

nourishing summer vegetable soup

The summer harvest is one of my favorite times of the year. We grow a small family garden at home, but we rely heavily on our local farmers' markets during the summer months. When you take advantage of those in-season prices, you really can save your budget while enjoying the flavors of the season.

Rich in flavor, this summer vegetable soup really has endless possibilities! Get the kids out to the farmers' market or out in the community gardens and let them pick the vegetables that will be in the soup. Don't underestimate what even the very little ones are learning; when children have been going to the fresh produce market since they could be in a baby carrier, it just becomes a part of them!

yield: 3 quarts (3 L)

$\frac{1}{3}$ cup (75 g) friendly fat to cook in, such as butter, tallow, lard, coconut oil or avocado oil

2 medium onions, diced

3 medium carrots, diced

3 cups (450 g) cut green beans

1 small yellow summer squash, chopped

1 medium zucchini, chopped

4-5 small red or yellow potatoes, chopped

Sea salt to taste

1 large tomato, seeded, juices scooped out and chopped

5 large cloves garlic, minced

1½ quarts (1.5 L) bone broth (see bone broth recipe on page 184)

1 tbsp (3 g) fresh chopped basil or 2 tsp (1.5 g) dried basil

Pepper to taste

Grated Parmesan cheese to garnish (optional)

Melt the friendly fat in a large soup or stockpot and toss in the onion, carrot, green beans, yellow squash, zucchini and potatoes and add a big pinch of sea salt to the vegetables. Cook over medium/medium-high heat, stirring occasionally for about 15 minutes or so. This low and slow sauté with sea salt will bring out all the juices in the veggies and sweeten them up.

Add the tomato and cook 5 minutes to bring out the juice. Add the garlic and cook for a minute.

Add the bone broth and basil, bring to a simmer and cook for 5 to 10 minutes.

Season to taste with sea salt and pepper. You can garnish each bowl with grated Parmesan if you wish. Serve baby about a tablespoon (15 ml) or so of soup right from the spoon to start with. You can completely puree the soup for babies who aren't handling pieces of soft vegetable yet.

You can store leftovers in the fridge for 5 to 7 days, or in the freezer for months.

note: When baby is over the age of 1 year, a cup or two (150-300 g) of summer corn is a delicious addition to this soup. Keep in mind that corn is a grain, so it is best to omit it until after baby is a year old. Add it with the onion, carrot and other veggies.

fresh spring vegetable soup

There is nothing like seeing those first spring vegetables start popping up at the farmers' markets! This soup is perfect for those cool first days of early spring! This is a good choice when you are ready for a seasonal veggie change after a long winter, and this fresh spring soup is loaded with spring asparagus, leeks and dill and garnished with fresh spring chives.

yield: 2 quarts (2 L)

¼ cup (57 g) friendly fat to cook in, such as butter, tallow, lard, coconut oil or avocado oil

1 large leek, halved, sliced and rinsed of sand

1 medium carrot, diced

¼ lb (113 g) mushrooms, sliced

2 small to medium russet potatoes, diced

Sea salt to taste

4 cloves garlic, minced

½ lb (230 g) fresh asparagus, hard and bitter ends discarded, cut on the bias into bite-sized pieces

1 tbsp (5–10 g) flour of choice to thicken (optional)

1½ quarts (1.5 L) bone broth (see bone broth recipe on page 184)

1 tsp dried parsley

½ tsp dried dill

Pepper to taste

Fresh chopped chives and raw cheese to garnish

Melt the friendly fat in a soup pot, add the leek, carrot, mushrooms and potatoes with a big pinch of sea salt to soften and sweeten the veggies. Cook the veggies over medium heat for about 10 minutes until everything gets soft and almost caramelizes.

Add the garlic and asparagus, and cook 5 minutes until the asparagus is bite-tender but still bright green.

Put the flour in if you choose to use it, stir to incorporate and cook for a minute.

Add the bone broth and seasoning and bring to a low simmer for 5 to 10 minutes. Serve with fresh chopped chives and slices of fresh raw cheese to garnish.

Serve baby about a tablespoon (15 ml) or so of soup right off the spoon to start with. You can completely puree the soup for babies who aren't yet handling pieces of soft vegetable.

notes: The flour is optional as the soup is delicious without it as well. If baby is under age 1 and has a grain-free diet, you can use tapioca or arrowroot starches. If the family tolerates grain and baby is over age 1, you can use white rice flour.

Sometimes I like to add a splash of white wine to deglaze the pan when the bone broth is added for additional flavor. The alcohol is cooked off, leaving behind delicious and rich flavor.

Sliced radishes work in this soup as well and are very pretty!

nutrient-dense green soup

This super smooth and creamy green soup is a powerhouse of vitamins and minerals! Loaded with gelatin-rich bone broth and mineral-packed spinach, it will give any lunch or dinner a nourishing punch. It is a fantastic, gentle way to introduce your baby to spinach, and the whole family will really like the taste.

In this soup, I absolutely love to make part of the fat some leftover bacon grease. The flavor makes this soup amazing! Spinach just goes so well with bacon, and the friendly fat that you use in the soup will allow all of those fat-soluble nutrients to be absorbed and digested well.

yield: 5 quarts (5 L)

$1/3$ cup (75 g) friendly fat to cook in, such as butter, leftover bacon grease, tallow, lard, coconut oil or avocado oil

2 medium onions, sliced

3 large carrots, coarsely chopped

3–4 yellow potatoes, cubed

Sea salt to taste

4–5 cloves garlic, coarsely chopped

2 quarts (2 L) bone broth
(see bone broth recipe on page 184)

1 lb (450 g) baby spinach

2 cups (475 ml) raw milk or coconut milk
(see coconut milk recipe on page 62)

Pepper to taste

Melt the friendly fat in a large soup or stockpot, and add the onion, carrot and potato with a large pinch of sea salt to bring out their juices and sweeten them. Cook on medium heat for about 10 minutes, stirring occasionally until everything softens.

Add the garlic and cook for a minute.

Turn up the heat, add the bone broth and bring to a simmer. Then add the spinach to cook for about 3 or 4 minutes. The spinach will wilt and turn bright green.

Turn off the heat, add the raw milk and use an immersion blender to puree the soup completely. You could transfer the soup to a regular blender to puree as well. Season with salt and pepper to taste. Serve baby about a tablespoon (15 ml) or so of soup right off the spoon to start with. You can use a straw for older babies and toddlers if that works better for them.

You can store leftovers in the fridge for 5 to 7 days, or in the freezer for months.

*See photo on page 74.

note: White sweet potatoes work well as a different option for the yellow potatoes in this recipe. If you have them available, you can use 1 medium-sized white sweet potato for this recipe.

creamy potato and leek soup

Few things are more comforting than a warm bowl of potato soup on a snowy day. My family really loves this version that we enjoy every winter, and I really love the ingredients. Leeks are available from the end of summer right through wintertime so it is easy to find everything here, and the leeks give a light, fresh onion flavor to the creamy soup.

Kids young and old love this one because it is so creamy and you will love that feeling of all that nourishing bone-broth being slurped up!

yield: 3-4 quarts (3-4 L)

$\frac{1}{3}$ cup (75 g) friendly fat to cook in, such as butter, tallow, lard, coconut oil or avocado oil

5 medium to large organic potatoes, cubed

4 organic leeks, sliced and rinsed of sand

Sea salt to taste

3 cloves garlic, coarsely chopped

2 quarts (2 L) bone broth
(see bone broth recipe on page 184)

1$\frac{1}{2}$ tsp (1.5 g) dried thyme leaves

Pepper to taste

Chopped chives to garnish (optional)

In a large soup pot, melt the friendly fat and add the potatoes and leeks with a large pinch of sea salt. Combine and cook on medium for about 10 minutes until the potatoes are fork-tender and the sea salt has drawn out the juices and sweetened the leeks.

Add the garlic and cook for a minute.

Add the bone broth and thyme, and bring to a simmer for about 5 minutes.

Turn the heat off, and use an immersion blender right in the pot to puree the soup completely, or transfer to a regular blender to puree.

Add sea salt and pepper to taste and garnish each bowl with the chives, if you'd like. Serve baby about a tablespoon (15 ml) or so of soup right off the spoon to start with. You can use a straw for older babies and toddlers if that works better for them.

note: You can store leftovers in the fridge for 5 to 7 days, or in the freezer for months. It is so nice to put half of the soup into the freezer to pull out on a busy day when you don't have time to cook!

part 2

nourishing meal ideas for the whole family & babies over 6 to 9 months

Once you have determined that baby is tolerating single foods well and responds positively to the more flavorful simple soups from Part 1, it's time to introduce a greater variety of textures and flavors. And mealtime gets even simpler for you!

The meals in this section are some of our family's favorite staples that are both delicious and super nutrient-dense so the whole family can sit down and eat together. These selections are meant to be your inspiration! If you have certain tastes or meals that you enjoy in your family culture, definitely introduce those to baby.

In Part 2, we are still keeping in mind that babies do not tolerate grains, nuts, legumes or egg whites until well after the age of 1, so these recipes are safe for babies who still need to avoid those items. You can easily add a grain to your plate if you wish, as your baby grows into toddlerhood and is ready for these items! Our focus in this part is nourishing and nutrient-dense foods, as well as keeping with our goal of creating a broad, adventurous palate in baby.

chapter 6

breakfast

Delicious for the whole family and designed for babies 6 to 9 months and older (free of grains, nuts, legumes, egg whites and sugar), these yummy breakfasts will give a supercharged start to the day!

From mineral-rich eggs and hashes loaded with vegetables to power-packed smoothies, you can start your family's day on the right foot. With lots of ideas and tips about how to make these breakfasts work on busy mornings, these meals can be done any day of the week.

nutrient-dense vegetable breakfast porridge

These power-packed breakfast bowls became my answer to a crabby baby who wanted her big sisters' oatmeal at the table! Since it is best to keep babies under age 1 away from grains like oats, I created a "porridge" that my babies and toddlers could have to feel like everyone else eating at the table.

This is creamy and mildly sweet and as big kids, my children still ask for this at breakfast!

yield: 4 to 5 kid servings

2 cups (510 g) cooked sweet potato or squash, pureed

¼ cup (18 g) unsweetened shredded coconut

4 soft or hard-boiled pastured egg yolks (yolk only)

2 tbsp (30 g) butter or coconut butter (see coconut butter recipe on page 189)

¼ cup (60 ml) whole yogurt or kefir

2 tsp (9 g) cold-soluble grass-fed gelatin

1–2 tbsp (5-10 ml) blackstrap molasses

Pinch of sea salt

Chopped crispy nuts or seeds of any kind (optional, for adults, children or babies over 1 year only)

Put everything but the nuts into a medium pot over low heat to combine and warm through.

Add the chopped nuts or seeds to the bowls of those who can have them. Serve baby a tablespoon (15 ml) to start, right from a spoon.

Leftovers can be stored in the fridge for 1 day. You can add the leftovers to a smoothie later the same day or the next morning.

notes: If baby is over 1 year, raw honey can be used instead of the molasses. Fruit puree works well for sweetening, too. Use fruit such as apples, pears or bananas.

When my family included both babies and big kids, I would set up small bowls of the chopped nuts and seeds for my big kids to add to their bowl like a buffet! Then the nuts and seeds wouldn't get added to baby's bowl.

This meal comes together really quickly if you have served the squash for dinner the night before.

veggie-loaded egg scramble

Colorful, mineral-rich vegetables meet nutrient-dense pastured eggs in this quick weekday breakfast for the whole family!

You can play around with the vegetable selection as to what is in season in your area. It will save your budget, and it will also keep the food-choice changing (which is good for our guts), as well as provide variety so we don't get bored with eating the same thing. It is a great way to clear out the veggie bin before grocery day!

yield: 2 adult and 3 small children servings

3 tbsp (43 g) friendly fat to cook in, such as butter, tallow, lard, coconut oil or avocado oil

½ medium onion, diced

2 cups (300 g) chopped seasonal vegetables such as bell peppers, zucchini, asparagus, carrots or greens

Sea salt to taste

1 clove garlic, minced

6 pastured eggs, whisked

1 tsp dried thyme leaves

Pepper to taste

Melt the friendly fat in a large skillet, and add the onion and veggies with a big pinch of sea salt to bring out their juices and sweeten them. Cook on medium heat until the vegetables are fork-tender and bright in color. This time will vary depending on the vegetable. Spinach cooks in just a couple of minutes, whereas carrots and asparagus will cook in 10 minutes or so.

Add the garlic and cook for a minute. Add the whisked eggs and thyme and combine. Please note: babies under age 1 year should not eat egg whites. If you have babies under age 1, you will need to set aside a bit of the cooked vegetables just for them so you can scramble an egg for baby with only the yolk instead of the whole egg. You can use a separate, smaller skillet on the next burner.

Stir the egg and veggie mixture until the eggs are cooked to your liking and then add salt and pepper to taste. This is a great finger-food meal for babies ready to pick up a soft piece of food to eat. For the younger ones, you can mash the eggs with the back of your fork, or puree with a little water or milk.

notes: This usually feeds my family of five, and I like to serve it with a glass of raw milk and a serving of fruit to complete the breakfast. Sometimes I add a slice of pastured bacon or sausage as well, or top the scramble with raw grated cheese.

To find sources of pastured eggs, ask around at your farmers' markets and local Weston A. Price Foundation chapters, or search the Eat Wild website online.

nourishing berries and greens smoothies

This quick, delicious smoothie is perfect for busy mornings—or teething babies and toddlers who don't want to chew! Smoothies are my go-to during those teething phases and you can pack so much nutrient punch in them!

Greens like spinach and kale are fantastic mineral sources; however, eating them raw can be tough on digestion. Greens like these digest best in cooked form and served with plenty of friendly fat, which also helps their fat-soluble nutrients be absorbed. I keep a container of steamed spinach or kale in the fridge to add to a quick smoothie, or you can quickly steam right before you make the smoothie.

yield: 3 small-child servings

1½ cups (360 ml) raw milk, kefir or coconut milk (see coconut milk recipe on page 62)

1½ cups (225 g) frozen organic berries

⅓ cup (60 g) steamed spinach or kale

1½ tbsp (20 g) grass-fed cold-soluble gelatin

3 pastured egg yolks

1 tbsp (15 ml) avocado oil or melted coconut oil

Place everything in your blender, puree until smooth and serve. You can serve baby on a spoon if he or she hasn't caught on to using a straw yet.

notes: Freeze leftovers in ice pop molds or little paper cups with a straw or ice-pop stick for a great snack or teething aide.

If you are making this in a larger amount for you or an older child to share with baby, add 1–2 teaspoons (5–10 ml) of raw honey or pure maple syrup if you wish. Babies under 1 should not have honey.

It is important to use yolks from hens that have been on pasture from a trusted source if you plan to use the raw yolk. If you do not have a good source, or if you don't feel comfortable using raw yolks, simply omit this ingredient. You could use a teaspoon of avocado oil or olive oil for fat, or more cream.

tropical green smoothie

This is my very favorite "first green smoothie" to introduce! Not only does it taste like you are on a tropical island (yes please!), but it is super gentle for baby to digest.

Mangos are mildly sweet and low in pectin for easy digestion in the raw state. And the amylase in the banana aids in digestion as well. Get a load of nutrition in one shot for the whole family on a busy morning! And your teething babies will love this one on their sore gums.

yield: 3 small-child servings

1½ cups (360 ml) coconut milk
(see coconut milk recipe on page 62)

1 cup (150 g) frozen organic mango

1 frozen banana

⅓ cup (60 g) steamed spinach

1½ tbsp (20 g) grass-fed cold-soluble gelatin

3 pastured egg yolks

1 tbsp (15 ml) melted coconut oil

Put everything in your blender, puree until smooth and serve. You can serve baby with a spoon if he or she hasn't caught on to using a straw yet.

Freeze leftovers in ice-pop molds or little paper cups with a straw or ice-pop stick for a great snack or teething aide.

notes: Raw milk or kefir work as substitutes for the coconut milk, if you don't have that around. Avocado oil works well as a substitute for the coconut oil if you don't care for coconut flavor.

If you are making this in a larger amount for you or an older child, add a teaspoon or two (5 to 10 ml) of raw honey or pure maple syrup if you wish. But remember that babies under 1 should not have honey.

It is important to use yolks from hens that have been on pasture from a trusted source if you plan to use the raw yolk. If you do not have a good source, or if you don't feel comfortable using raw yolks, simply omit this ingredient. You could use a teaspoon of avocado oil or olive oil for fat, or more cream.

colorful veggie breakfast hash

Vegetable hashes are one of my "go-to" breakfast items when I don't want to think too much. They also serve as a fantastic way to do a fridge veggie bin "clean out" at the end of the week! I am giving my favorite flavor combination in this recipe, but certainly use what is in season for you—and what needs to be used up!

yield: 2 adult and 3 small-child servings

¼ cup (57 g) friendly fat to cook in, such as butter, lard, tallow, coconut oil or avocado oil

1 small onion, diced

2 medium potatoes, diced

1 medium sweet potato, diced

Sea salt to taste

1 small yellow bell pepper, diced

1 small red bell pepper, diced

2 medium zucchini, diced

3 large cloves of garlic, minced

1 tsp red pepper flakes, or more if you like the heat

Pepper to taste

3 tbsp (43 g) butter

5 pastured eggs

Fresh green onion or chopped parsley to garnish (optional)

Melt the friendly fat in your large skillet, add the onion, potatoes and sweet potatoes with a big pinch of sea salt, and cook over medium heat for about 7 to 10 minutes until the vegetables are slightly browned and soft.

Add the bell peppers, zucchini, garlic and red pepper flakes and cook until those veggies are bite-tender, about 5 minutes. You can cook them longer if you want them softer. Add sea salt and pepper to taste and top with fried eggs (yolk-only for babies under age 1 year).

To fry the eggs, you can melt 3 tablespoons (45 g) butter in a skillet, and once melted add 5 eggs. Cook over medium heat until they are cooked to your yolk preference. This is a great finger-food meal for those ready to pick up soft pieces of food to eat. For the younger ones, you can mash the eggs with the back of your fork, or puree with a little water or milk.

note: I like to serve any hash topped with a fried egg. (Make sure to use only the yolk for babies under 1 year.) When that warm yolk runs into the hash, it is just so good! You can certainly serve it with pastured bacon or sausage instead. I even like to put a small dish of whole yogurt topped with fruit on the plate as well.

sweet potato and greens breakfast sauté

This satisfying, nutrient-dense breakfast will quickly become a family favorite, and it will quickly become *your* favorite as you get a big load of mineral-rich greens to the family in one sitting!

We know a loving family who raise pigs on pasture for us every year, and we really enjoy our pork. I season my ground pork with my own sausage seasoning blend. The flavors of the sausage blend into the greens and sweet potatoes and make for such a flavorful breakfast.

yield: 2 adult and 3 small-child servings

½ tsp sea salt, plus more to taste

¼ tsp garlic powder

¼ tsp onion powder

¼ tsp dried basil

¼ tsp dried thyme leaves

⅛ tsp cumin

⅛ tsp dried marjoram

⅛ tsp black pepper, plus more to taste

Pinch of cayenne pepper

½ lb (230 g) pastured ground pork

1 tbsp (14 g) butter

½ medium onion, chopped

2 large sweet potatoes, cut into small cubes

3 cloves garlic, minced

½ lb (230 g) organic baby spinach or de-ribbed and chopped kale

In a small mixing bowl, whisk the sea salt, garlic powder, onion powder, basil, thyme, cumin, marjoram, pepper and cayenne to combine, and then mix this sausage seasoning blend into the ground pork.

Warm a skillet to medium-high heat, melt a tablespoon (15 g) of butter and crumble the sausage meat into the pan. Brown the sausage until it is cooked through and no longer pink. Set the cooked sausage aside. Leave some of the sausage fat in the pan to cook some of the other ingredients, or you can add a couple of tablespoons of butter instead.

Cook the onion and sweet potato with a few pinches of sea salt over medium heat for about 10 minutes. You can add a splash of water to the pan if it is getting dry. You want the sweet potatoes to get soft and slightly caramelized.

Add the garlic and cook for a minute. Add the spinach and cooked sausage and cook until the spinach wilts, and then add sea salt and pepper to taste. This is a great finger-food meal for those babies ready to pick up a soft piece of food to eat. For the younger ones, you can mash the sausage with the back of your fork, or puree with a little water or milk.

notes: You can use a prepared ground pork sausage instead of making your own seasoning blend if you wish. Just really watch the ingredient lists. There can very easily be hidden MSG in sausage products, even from a butcher. To find sources of pastured pork, ask around at your farmer's markets and local Weston A. Price Foundation chapters, or search the Eat Wild website online.

Grass-fed beef works as a substitute if you don't have access to quality sourced pork. If your older babies can handle it, 5 to 6 strips of bacon chopped up work really well as something different, too. My babies could handle chopped up bacon when they were around 1 year old.

hashbrowns and greens with fried eggs

One of the things I had to get used to in my real-food journey was having vegetables for breakfast. While veggies aren't as important as friendly fats for growing babies, I wanted to be sure I got them used to vegetables being served at most meals of the day because, in all truth, they really are that important as we get older! Filled with the mineral punch we need, vegetables really would have been eaten in traditional cultures more than just dinnertime.

I just love hash browns, and you will never taste the spinach in this hash—promise! This meal is our Saturday morning staple every weekend, and that tradition is one my girls have grown to look forward to.

yield: 2 adult and 3 small-child servings

$1/3$ cup (75 g) friendly fat to cook in, such as butter, tallow, lard, coconut oil or avocado oil

4 medium potatoes, cubed small

2 tsp (10 g) sea salt, plus more to taste

$1/2$ tsp ground pepper, plus more to taste

1 tsp onion powder

1 tsp garlic powder

$1/2$ lb (230 g) organic baby spinach, chopped fine

6 pastured eggs, or however many eggs your family will eat

Melt the friendly fat in a large skillet and add the potatoes along with all of the seasonings. Stir to combine and cook on medium or medium-low heat for about 20 minutes, stirring only occasionally so the sides of the cubed potatoes can brown well. The potatoes will get soft on the inside and crispy on the outside. Add more fat if you feel like the pan is getting dry, but $1/3$ cup (80 ml) should do.

Add the chopped spinach and cook until it is wilted, which is just a few minutes. You can cook it longer if you want the spinach to get "crispy." Either way, the finely chopped spinach really wilts down and you will barely notice it!

Once the hash is almost finished cooking, you can fry your eggs, over easy or however you like them, in a separate skillet. (Make sure to use only the yolk for babies under 1 year old.) Add additional sea salt and pepper to your hash and eggs as you wish.

This is a great finger food meal for those babies ready to pick up soft pieces of food to eat. For the younger ones, you can mash the eggs with the back of your fork, or puree with a little water or milk.

*See photo on page 101.

notes: I like to serve this breakfast with a glass of raw milk and a piece of fruit. This serves my family of 5 for one breakfast. You can warm any leftover hash for breakfast or lunch the next day.

This is such a quick recipe that I sometimes even serve this on school mornings! The potatoes can be chopped up really fast and don't need a lot of hands-on time once they are in the pan; it really comes together fast, and everyone can have a warm breakfast before school.

chapter 7

lunch & dinner

This chapter includes great meal ideas that work for both lunch and dinner to serve for the whole family but that are also designed for babies 6 to 9 months and older (free of grains, nuts, legumes, egg whites and sugar). With lots of ideas and tips on how to make these recipes work on busy weekdays, you can make nourishing stews and nutrient-dense, refueling meals even on work and school days.

nourishing pastured chicken stew

There is so much comforting flavor in one warm bowl of soup! Adding pureed squash to a pot of soup is one of my tricks to get a lightly creamy and flavorful broth as well as beautiful color. This stew will become a family favorite and is perfect for packing as leftovers in a thermos for work or school the next day.

yield: 4 quarts (4 L)

---

2 acorn squashes

2 medium onions, chopped

4 medium carrots, chopped

4 stalks celery, chopped

2 medium potatoes, chopped

$\frac{1}{3}$ cup (75 g) friendly fat to cook in, such as butter, tallow, lard, coconut oil or avocado oil

Sea salt to taste

1 head garlic, about 8 cloves, minced

2 quarts (2 L) chicken bone broth (see bone broth recipe on page 184)

2 cups (250 g) cooked chicken, shredded (see slow cooker chicken page 36 or roasted chicken page 116)

$\frac{1}{8}$–$\frac{1}{4}$ tsp cayenne pepper

$\frac{1}{4}$–$\frac{1}{2}$ lb (113–230 g) fresh organic baby spinach

Pepper to taste

Put the acorn squashes in the oven on a baking sheet, whole, at 425°F (220°C) for 1 hour. When you take them out, cut them in half and let them cool to the touch while you start making the soup.

Sauté the onion, carrot, celery and potatoes in the butter with a few big pinches of sea salt to bring out their juices and sweeten. Cook on medium heat for about 10 minutes.

While the veggies are cooking, scoop out the squash from the shell and puree the flesh in your processor or blender with a little of the bone broth to be sure it gets fully pureed.

Add the garlic to the pot and cook for a minute. Add the squash puree, bone broth, chicken and cayenne to the pot and simmer for about 5 minutes. Add the spinach to wilt and then season with sea salt and pepper to taste.

Serve the stew to baby on a spoon. If baby isn't handling bits of soft vegetables yet, you can puree his or her portion so it is smooth or semi-smooth.

notes: I like to thicken my stew with tapioca or sometimes white rice flour. Tapioca is grain-free flour made from the cassava root vegetable. It is safe for grain-free diets for babies so you can use it if you have little ones under age 1. Use about $\frac{1}{4}$ cup (30 g)—stir it up with a little water before adding to the soup pot—stirring it in at the end with the spinach. If you tolerate grains and have toddlers that can as well, you can use white rice flour or sprouted brown rice flour. If you and your family tolerate gluten, you could use a sprouted wheat flour.

This recipe makes enough soup for my family for about three or so lunches or dinners. You can freeze leftover soup if you want, pack it up in school or work lunch thermoses the next day or serve it for the next day's meal.

hearty slow-cooker beef stew with marrow

The ultimate fall and winter comfort meal—slow-cooker style! This saucy, flavorful stew is my favorite way to use leftover, nutrient-dense grass-fed marrow from bones used for making beef broth. I freeze the marrow and chop it into this stew when I am ready to make it. You really don't see or taste the marrow, but it sure does boost the nutrition!

Note that this recipe will need to be planned in advance, allowing 12 to 24 hours for the beef to marinate.

yield: 3 quarts (3 L)

2 lbs (900 g) grass-fed beef stew meat or roast, cubed into bite-sized pieces

3 cups (700 ml) quality red wine

3 cloves smashed garlic

3 bay leaves

1 cup (122 g) arrowroot or tapioca flour

2 tsp (10 ml) sea salt, plus more to taste

1 tsp pepper, plus more to taste

3-4 tbsp (45-60 g) butter

4-5 carrots, chopped

4-5 celery, chopped

2 onion, chopped

2 large tomatoes, seeds and juices scooped out, and chopped

5 small yellow or red potatoes, chopped

4 cloves garlic, minced

¼ cup (51 g) grass-fed marrow from beef bones, chopped finely or pureed (see bone broth recipe on page 184)

2-3 cups (475 -700 ml) beef bone broth (see bone broth recipe on page 184)

Combine the beef, wine, garlic and bay leaves in a container with a lid and set in the fridge to marinate 12 to 24 hours. After it has marinated, strain the meat but set 2 cups (475 ml) of the marinade aside for later.

Combine the arrowroot, sea salt and pepper in a small mixing bowl. Coat the meat in the arrowroot mixture and sear it in butter in a hot skillet, about 3 to 4 minutes. Just sear the sides to give it a beautiful, golden brown crust. The middle will not be cooked through but it will finish in the slow cooker.

Once the meat is seared, put it in your slow cooker, add the reserved red wine marinade to the searing pan and bring to a simmer. Scrape up any bits from cooking the meat, and then pour this sauce into the slow cooker. Add the rest of the ingredients to the slow cooker, stir to combine and cook on low for 8 to 10 hours. Season with salt and pepper to taste.

Serve the stew to baby with a spoon, making sure that the stew meat is cut up well. You can pulse the stew in a blender to make it easier for younger ones still learning how to manage meat.

Store leftovers in the fridge for 5 days. This stew freezes very well for up to 6 months and makes for the perfect quick pull-out dinner on a busy night.

notes: The wine really does give a depth of flavor that I love and the alcohol is cooked off. If you don't keep wine in the house, you can use a hearty seasoned beef broth for the marinade instead.

Tapioca and arrowroot flours are grain-free flours made from the cassava root plant. These are safe for babies under 1 year old. If your family tolerates grains you can use white rice flour or a sprouted brown rice flour. If you tolerate gluten, you could use a sprouted wheat flour (such as Einkorn) for the coating on the meat. These flours thicken the stew for the saucy feel you want in a stew broth.

nutrient-dense grass-fed beef and liver meatballs with bone-broth gravy

One meal that I remember from my childhood is meatballs and gravy. With a few real-food tweaks, I've taken one of my favorite childhood comfort dinners and made it into a nutrient-dense, nourishing dinner for the whole family!

yield: 2 adult and 3 small-child servings, with a little leftover

---

for the meatballs

1 lb (450 g) grass-fed ground beef

1/4 cup (55 g) grated or finely chopped liver

1/4 medium onion, finely chopped

1/4 medium green pepper, finely chopped

2 cloves garlic, minced

1 tsp sea salt

1/4 tsp pepper

2 pastured egg yolks (or if baby is over 1 year use 1 whole egg)

1/4 cup (32 g) tapioca or arrowroot flour

for the bone broth gravy

2 tbsp (30 g) butter

2-3 tbsp (15-23 g) tapioca flour, depending on how thick you like your gravy

1 pint (475 ml) bone broth (see bone broth recipe on page 184)

1 tsp dried thyme leaves

Sea salt and pepper to taste

Preheat your oven to 375°F (190°C).

Put all of the meatball ingredients into a medium mixing bowl, combine well with your hands and roll the meat mixture into meatballs about the size of ping pong balls. Set the meatballs close together onto a silicone baking mat or parchment paper on a baking sheet.

Bake the meatballs in the oven at 375°F (190°C) for 30 to 35 minutes until the tops are golden brown. While the meatballs are baking, you can make your gravy.

To make the bone broth gravy, melt the butter over medium-high heat in a saucepan, add the flour and stir with a whisk to combine. Add the bone broth and thyme and bring to a simmer, stirring occasionally with your whisk until the mixture thickens. Season the gravy with salt and pepper to taste. The gravy only takes about 5 minutes to make!

Add the meatballs to the gravy, combine and serve alongside a vegetable side dish. Serve the meatballs to baby cut up into finger-food-sized meat pieces. They are soft and quite easy to handle, but you could also pulse them in the blender with some of the gravy for the little ones who cannot yet manage finger foods.

notes: When making the gravy, start with less flour; you can always add more in the end if you want the gravy to be thicker. If the gravy turns out thicker than you want, you can thin it with more broth or even water.

I like to serve this dinner with garlic mashed potatoes or sweet potatoes, and steamed broccoli or green beans. It is just like it was when I had it as a kid!

zucchini "noodle" spaghetti with grass-fed mini meatballs

It doesn't get much more fun than serving little ones their first spaghetti meal! Those saucy faces are something you will never forget. Just plan for bath time after dinner! Using veggie "noodles" instead of grain-based noodles makes this a safe option for families with babies not eating grains yet, and is a nice way to change up spaghetti night by adding more veggies to everyone's plates.

yield: 2 adult and 3 small-child servings, with a little leftover

---

1 lb (450 g) grass-fed ground beef

2 tsp (10 g) sea salt, plus more to taste

½ tsp ground pepper, plus more to taste

1 tbsp (2 g) Italian seasoning

3 tbsp (45 g) friendly fat to cook in such as butter, tallow, lard, coconut oil or avocado oil

1 medium onion, chopped

1 large green pepper, chopped

½ lb (230 g) organic mushrooms, sliced

5 cloves garlic, minced

1 jar organic spaghetti sauce

3–4 large zucchinis, sliced into noodles through a spiralizer

Freshly chopped basil and grated raw cheese to garnish

Preheat the oven to 350°F (175°C).

Mix the beef, salt, pepper and Italian seasoning in a small mixing bowl. Using your hands works best.

Roll the seasoned beef into small balls. I like to make them about the size of a large marble. Set them close together on a silicone baking mat or parchment paper on a baking sheet, and bake them at 350°F (175°C) for 15 minutes.

Melt the friendly fat in a pot, add the onion, green pepper and mushrooms with a big pinch of sea salt and cook on medium heat for 10 minutes until everything softens and sweetens.

Add the garlic to the pot of cooked veggies and cook for a minute. Add the spaghetti sauce and cooked mini meatballs, bring the sauce to a low simmer, put the lid on and simmer the sauce for about 10 minutes. Season the sauce with salt and pepper to taste.

To make the zucchini noodles, add the spiralized zucchini to a pot of boiling water, boil for about 3 minutes and then strain. Alternatively, you could do a quick sauté of the zucchini noodles in a skillet for about 3 minutes with a tablespoon (15 g) of butter and small pinch of sea salt. Either way, let the noodles drain for at least 5 minutes in a strainer to get all the water out or your sauce will get watery. Plate your zucchini noodles, ladle sauce with meatballs over the top and garnish with fresh basil and grated raw cheese.

Serve to baby finger-food style, making sure the zucchini noodles are cut up and not too long. You could pulse this dish in the blender a little if you wish, though the zucchini noodles are always a big finger-food hit!

note: Zucchini noodles have a fantastic "noodle feel" and can be used while baby is still too young to have grain. When your toddler is ready to have grain, you can use rice noodles, or, if gluten is not a problem, wheat noodles.

italian stuffed spaghetti squash

You can stuff just about any sort of squash, but I think this is my very favorite way to do it. A fantastic grain-free way to enjoy a lasagna-type dinner as a whole family—including baby! What kid doesn't love goopy, melty cheese!

yield: 2 adult and 3 small-child servings, with a little leftover

1 large spaghetti squash, halved, with seeds scooped out

$1/3$ cup (70 g) butter, divided

6 cloves garlic, minced, divided

1 tsp sea salt

$1/4$ tsp ground pepper

2–4 tsp (3–6 g) Italian seasoning, divided

$2/3$ cup (160 ml) organic spaghetti sauce, divided

1 lb (450 g) ground pastured pork sausage

1 medium onion, diced

5 cups (335 g) chopped kale

$1 1/2$–2 cups (150–200 g) freshly grated Parmesan or other raw cheese, divided

Freshly chopped basil to garnish

Preheat the oven to 425°F (220°C).

Spread about $1/4$ cup (60 g) butter over the flesh of the squash, and season with sea salt, pepper, 2 cloves of minced garlic and 2 teaspoons (3 g) Italian seasoning. Then divide $1/3$ cup (80 ml) of the spaghetti sauce between the squash halves, filling the cavities. Roast the spaghetti squash, flesh-side up, in the oven at 425°F (220°C) for 1 hour.

About 20 minutes before the squash is finished roasting, you can make your filling. Melt 2 to 3 tablespoons (30 to 45 g) of butter in a large skillet and add the ground sausage. If you are using un-seasoned sausage, add 1 to 2 teaspoons (1.5 to 3 g) Italian seasoning. Add the rest of the minced garlic. Cook over medium-high heat until the meat is cooked through.

Add the diced onions and chopped kale and cook over medium heat about 7 minutes until the kale is bright green and cooked.

Put $1/2$ to 1 cup (50 to 100 g) of cheese over the roasted squash, and then divide the meat and kale mixture over the cheese. Divide the remaining $1/3$ cup (80 ml) spaghetti sauce over the top of the filling on each squash half, top with an additional 1 cup (100 g) of cheese, and cook 5 to 7 minutes in the oven at 425°F (220°C) until the cheese is bubbly and melted.

To serve, use a fork to pull out some of the spaghetti squash with the filling. Top with freshly chopped basil. Serve to baby on a spoon or finger-food style. You could pulse this in a blender if baby isn't handling pieces of soft veggies yet.

notes: You can use grass-fed ground beef instead of the pork sausage if you'd like. To season, use 2 teaspoons (3 g) Italian seasoning, 1 teaspoon cumin and $1/8$ teaspoon cayenne pepper.

This serves my family of five for one dinner plus leftovers for a few smaller lunches or dinners.

chicken "zoodle" soup

Chicken soup is one of those childhood comfort meals. There is just something about the brothy, seasoned flavor in this soup that will make you melt back in your chair and relax. Babies love to learn how to handle this chicken "zoodle" soup with the fun veggie noodles, and you can feel really good about them happily getting a great serving or two of mineral-rich vegetables and bone broth.

yield: 3 quarts (3 L)

¼ cup (60 g) friendly fat to cook in such as butter, tallow, lard, coconut oil or avocado oil

2 medium onions

6 medium carrots, chopped

6 medium celery stalks, chopped

Sea salt to taste

5 large cloves garlic, minced

2 quarts (2 L) bone broth, plus more if needed (see bone broth recipe on page 184)

2 cups (250 g) cooked chicken (see the slow-cooker chicken recipe on page 36 or the roasted chicken recipe on page 116)

1 tsp all-purpose seasoning (such as Simply Organic brand)

¼–½ tsp cayenne (optional)

6 medium zucchinis, spiralized

Pepper to taste

Melt the friendly fat in your stockpot over medium heat. Then add the onion, carrot and celery with a big pinch of sea salt and cook slowly over medium heat for about 10 to 15 minutes to bring out their juices and sweeten them.

Add the garlic and cook for a minute, and then add the bone broth, chicken and seasoning and bring to a simmer.

Add the spiralized zucchini, and cook for about 3 to 5 minutes. It will seem like you need more liquid, but do not add more. The zucchini will release a lot of liquid once the salt gets to it and it cooks. You can always add more broth if you want a brothier soup, but wait the few minutes to see how much liquid comes off the zucchini first.

Serve the soup to baby on a spoon. While the soup can seem messy for babies to feed themselves, all of the components in the soup are very soft and easy for babies to manage. They learn by practicing, so I just plan for the mess and once they catch on, the feedings get less messy. You could pulse the soup in a blender to make it easier to manage for babies who aren't yet eating pieces of soft veggies.

This soup freezes well up to 6 months, and keeps well in the fridge for up to 5 days. It makes great lunchbox additions in a thermos.

butter- and thyme-roasted chicken with simple pan gravy

Chicken day is my favorite dinner day of the week. It may seem that roasting a chicken would be a lot of work for a weekday, but the hands-on time is so minimal. Butter and thyme are a match made in heaven for this crispy, salty, herby chicken skin that everyone will want their hands on!

yield: 2 adult and 3 small-child servings for 2 meals

---

for the roasted chicken

3 carrots, coarsely chopped

3 celery stalks, coarsely chopped

1 medium onion, coarsely chopped

3 cloves garlic, minced

2 cups (475 ml) white wine, bone broth or water

1 whole pastured chicken, about 6 lb (2.7 kg)

1–2 tbsp (15–30 g) butter

1 tsp sea salt

½ tsp ground pepper

1–2 tsp (1–2 g) dried thyme

for the gravy

2 tbsp (30 g) butter

2 tbsp (14 g) tapioca flour

2 cups (475 ml) strained pan juices from cooking the chicken

1 tsp dried thyme

Sea salt or pepper to taste

Preheat the oven to 250°F (120°C).

Put the veggies in the bottom of your roasting pan along with the wine (or bone broth or water), tie up the legs of your chicken with cooking twine and place the chicken breast-down in the roasting pan. Cover and roast with the lid on at 250°F (120°C) for 3 hours.

After 3 hours, turn the chicken breast-side up, butter the skin and sprinkle with seasonings. Strain off 2 cups (475 ml) of the pan juices from the bottom of the roasting pan to use for the gravy. Roast the chicken for another 45 minutes with the lid off and with the heat turned up to 350°F (175°C). Remove the chicken from the oven and let it rest for a few minutes before carving.

To make the gravy, melt the butter in a saucepan, add the flour and stir with a whisk to combine. Add the strained liquid and bring to a simmer, stirring occasionally with a whisk until the gravy thickens. Season with salt and pepper to taste.

You can pulse the chicken, with the gravy or just the pan juices, for baby to eat. When baby starts enjoying finger foods at the table, you can shred or cut the pieces of meat very finely for him or her to enjoy.

notes: I like to serve this chicken with mashed potatoes or sweet potatoes and butter, and steamed or roasted broccoli.

The leftover meat is great to use in soups, stews, stir-fry dishes, salads or sandwiches. I can very easily use a whole chicken within a week for my family of five, but if you think you won't use it all within a few days, you can shred and freeze the meat. Be sure to save the carcass for making bone broth (see page 184). I usually put the bones right into my slow cooker as I am taking the chicken apart after dinner. You can freeze the bones if you don't wish to start your bone broth right away.

spatchcock herbed chicken

Now this is fast food, real-food style! While I absolutely love my slow-roasted chicken, sometimes time just doesn't allow for it. And in the blazing hot middle of summer, having the oven or slow cooker running all day isn't exactly the smartest cooking method.

Grab up some of your favorite fresh herbs and get ready for that buttery, crispy chicken in about an hour!

yield: 2 adult and 3 small-child servings for 2 meals
(or 1 meal with leftover chicken for use in other meals)

3-4 tbsp (45-60 g) butter for the bottom of the pan and surface of the chicken

1 onion, sliced into rounds

1 whole pastured chicken, split down the backbone spatchcock-style

2 cloves of garlic, minced

1 tsp sea salt

¼ tsp ground pepper

3-4 sprigs fresh thyme, finely chopped

3-4 sprigs fresh oregano, finely chopped

Preheat the oven to 425°F (220°C).

Butter the bottom of a large baking sheet or jellyroll pan, lay slices of onion on top, and the spatchcocked chicken on top of the onion rounds. Butter the surface of the chicken, rub in the minced garlic, and sprinkle with sea salt, pepper and fresh herbs.

Cook at 425°F (220°C) for 1 hour until the chicken is fully cooked and juices run clear. This quick spatchcock method locks in moisture fast and the meat is really tender.

You can pulse the chicken with bone broth or water for baby to eat. When baby starts enjoying finger foods at the table, you can shred or cut the pieces of meat very finely for him or her to enjoy. I had one baby who, by the age of 1 year, just flat out refused to be fed by me, so figuring out how to help her eat meat without my help was important! She managed finely shredded chicken very well.

notes: You can change the fresh herbs to use whatever is in season! I love using fresh dill weed in the summer. I like to serve this chicken with fresh salads, homemade dressings and quick roasted potatoes. You can serve baby a side of simple steamed veggies or soup.

The leftover meat is great to use in soups, stews, stir-fry dishes, salads or sandwiches. I can very easily use a whole chicken within a week for my family of five, but if you think you won't use it all within a few days, you can shred and freeze the meat so it keeps longer and then pull it out of the freezer as you need it.

Be sure to save the carcass for making bone broth (see page 184). I usually put the bones right into my slow cooker as I am taking the chicken apart after dinner. You can freeze the bones if you don't wish to start your bone broth right away.

herbed cauliflower "rice" & veggie bowls

This recipe became a staple in my house after I had my third baby. My older girls would often have veggie rice bowls with long grain white rice for lunch, and when my baby was at that age where she could pull herself up to chairs, she would sit at her sisters' sides begging for a bite!

Cauliflower "rice" looks and feels just like the rice grain, so I started making their rice bowls this way on occasion so that their little sister who was still under 1 year old could join in on the fun!

yield: 2 adult and 3 small-child servings

---

1 head of cauliflower

¼ cup (60 g) friendly fat, such as butter, tallow, lard, coconut oil or avocado oil

½ medium onion, diced

1 cup (128 g) diced carrots

1 cup (88 g) broccoli florets, sliced thin

1 cup (67 g) chopped kale

1 cup (134 g) peas

Sea salt to taste

3 cloves garlic, minced

2 tsp (2 g) dried thyme leaves

Pepper to taste

Grated Parmesan or other raw cheese to top (optional)

Chop the cauliflower into manageable-sized pieces for the food processor, and pulse to make "cauliflower rice." It is easiest to do half of the cauliflower head at a time. Set the cauliflower rice aside.

Melt the friendly fat in a large skillet and add the onion, carrots, broccoli, kale and peas. Toss to combine with a big pinch of sea salt and cook on medium heat for about 7 minutes until the veggies are bite-tender and bright in color.

Add the garlic, thyme, pepper and cauliflower rice and cook over medium heat for a few minutes until the cauliflower rice is bite-tender. If you cook it too long, it will get mushy. Garnish with grated raw cheese, if using.

Serve to baby right off the spoon or finger-food style. If baby isn't managing soft bits of cooked veggies yet, you could pulse it in the blender with some bone broth or water.

notes: Add cooked chicken, beef, lamb, pork, etc. if you like! I usually serve this as is for lunch with a topping of raw cheese. If I am serving this for dinner, I like to add meatballs. You could even add a fried pastured egg.

You can substitute some regular rice for the cauliflower rice if you have older toddlers eating grains safely.

Swap the veggies for what is in season: asparagus in the spring, zucchini in the summer! I also like to add fresh GMO-free corn from our local farmer. Remember corn is a grain and is not appropriate for babies who are not yet eating grains.

Increase the seasoning to your family's favorites! I like to give it a spicy cayenne or smoky paprika kick sometimes.

simple and quick pan-seared salmon with homemade tartar sauce

It is ironic that growing up around as many freshwater lakes as we have here, I really didn't have a taste for fish. It has taken me a while to train my palate for fish, and one of my goals with my little ones was to help them like fish from young ages!

The buttery, crispy skin on these salmon fillets will win over any non-lover of fish! And this super quick cook time will win over busy momma too! This makes a great meal for the whole family on busy weeknights.

yield: 2 adult and 3 small-child servings

---

for the tartar sauce

½ cup (120 ml) avocado oil or olive oil

½ cup (120 ml) whole sour cream

Juice of ½ lemon

3 tsp (15 ml) mustard

2 tsp (10 ml) raw honey (if baby is under 1 year use pure maple syrup instead)

½ tsp sea salt

½ tsp garlic powder

¼ tsp black pepper

¼ cup (40 g) chopped pickles

2–3 tbsp (30–45 ml) pickle juice

for the salmon

⅓ cup (80 g) butter, pastured lard, tallow or avocado oil

4–5 wild-caught salmon fillets

2 tsp (10 g) sea salt

½ tsp ground pepper

1–2 tsp (1–2 g) dried thyme leaves or other herb your family enjoys

¼–⅛ tsp cayenne pepper (optional)

Make the tartar sauce first. Put the avocado oil, sour cream, lemon juice, mustard, honey, sea salt, garlic powder and black pepper in a pint (473-ml) jar and use an immersion blender to blend until the mixture is thick and creamy. This will take less than a minute. Stir in the chopped pickles and pickle juice and set the tartar sauce aside in the refrigerator until the fish is ready.

Melt the butter in the bottom of a large skillet, and sprinkle both sides of the salmon fillets with the seasonings.

Put the salmon fillets in the skillet, skin-side down, and cook over medium-high heat for about 5 minutes until the skin is golden brown and crispy. You can let it go a little further if you like the skin really crispy.

Flip the salmon over and cook the other side about 4 to 5 minutes until golden brown. Let the fish rest with the heat off, then serve with the tartar sauce for dipping. To serve baby, you can cut finger-food- sized pieces of fish and drizzle the sauce over the top. Baby will watch how you dip and catch on to that fast, though! You could pulse the fish with the sauce in the blender a little if the baby isn't ready for bite-sized pieces.

*See photo on page 104.

notes: I like to serve this fish with roasted root vegetables or my Hearty Roasted Root Veggie Soup (page 84).

If we happen to have leftovers, they make great fish sandwiches the next day for lunch. For my babies, I would just make a fish salad by mixing the fish with some sour cream or leftover tartar sauce, and they would eat it with a spoon or by the fist full. My older kids will eat this fish salad in a lettuce wrap or rice wrap.

slow-cooker grass-fed beef roast 2 ways with pan gravy

You can fill your home with the aroma of a slow-cooked beef roast any night of the week with these two methods to pick from. If it is a slow, lazy weekend day at home, you can warm up the house with the oven for the afternoon, or if it is a busy weekday and everyone is away at school, work and day care, everyone can gather at the end of the day to enjoy a slow-cooker roast that has made the home smell amazing. This is truly a one-pot meal. The carrots and potatoes slow-cook right along with the beef for instant side dishes!

yield: 2 adult and 3 small-child servings for 2 meals

---

for the roast

About 3 lbs (1350 g) grass-fed chuck roast

1 onion, coarsely chopped

5 large carrots, cut lengthwise for serving

6 yellow or red potatoes, quartered

3-4 cups (700-950 ml) red wine, beef bone broth, water or a combination of any

3 cloves of garlic, minced

2-3 tsp (2-3 g) dried thyme leaves

1-2 tsp (5-10 g) sea salt

1 tsp ground pepper

for the pan gravy

2 tbsp (30 g) butter

2 tbsp (14 g) tapioca flour

2 cups (475 ml) strained pan juices from cooking the roast

Sea salt or pepper to taste

slow cooker method

Put the onion, carrot and potato into your slow cooker, and then put the roast on top. Pour the wine over the roast, sprinkle your seasonings and the minced garlic over the top of the roast and into the liquid as well. Sprinkle some of the seasoning over your veggies too. Put the lid on, and cook on low for 8 to 10 hours.

oven method

Preheat the oven to 275°F (135°C). Put the onion, carrot and potato into the bottom of a roasting pan, and then put the roast on top. Pour the wine over the roast, sprinkle your seasonings and the minced garlic over the top of the roast and sprinkle some into the liquid as well. Sprinkle some of the seasoning over your veggies too. Put the lid on the roasting pan, and slow-cook at 275°F (135°C) for 3 to 4 hours.

pan gravy

Melt the butter in a saucepan, add the flour and stir with a whisk to combine. Add the roasting liquid and bring to a simmer, stirring occasionally with your whisk until the mixture thickens. Season with salt and pepper to taste.

You can pulse the beef with the gravy or with just the liquid from the pan for baby to eat. When baby starts enjoying finger foods at the table, you can shred or cut the pieces of meat very finely for him or her to enjoy. I had one baby who, by the age of 1 year, just flat out refused to be fed, so figuring out how to help her eat meat without my help was important! She managed shredded beef just fine. These two methods of cooking provide very moist, fall-off-the-bone meat.

wild-caught tuna salad

Loaded with brain-fueling omega-3 fatty acids, tuna fish makes a great midday meal. Creating a love for tuna fish will make for easy lunch packing when the kids are at school ages. Find a great canned wild-caught, sustainable source (many conventional stores carry them these days) and tuna salad is just a few minutes away!

yield: 2 adult and 3 small-child servings

---

for the homemade mayonnaise

½ cup (120 ml) avocado oil (olive oil works too or a combination of the two)

½ cup (120 ml) whole sour cream

Juice of ½ lemon

2 tsp (10 ml) organic mustard

1 tsp sea salt

1 tsp garlic powder

½ tsp pepper

for the tuna salad

½ small or medium apple, quartered

2 stalks celery, quartered

2 medium carrots, quartered

3 (5-oz [142-g]) cans wild-caught tuna, drained

Sea salt and pepper to taste

To make the homemade mayonnaise, put the avocado oil, sour cream, lemon juice, mustard, sea salt, garlic powder and pepper in a pint (473-ml) jar and blend with an immersion blender for about a minute until it thickens.

Put the apple, celery, carrot and tuna into your food processor and pulse into a medium chop. (If you don't have a food processor, just chop the veggies and crush the nuts.)

Put the homemade mayo, chopped apple, carrot, celery and the tuna in a medium mixing bowl, combine well and season with sea salt and pepper to taste.

If you have really little ones, you can put the tuna salad in your food processor or blender and puree. I still have one little one who prefers her tuna salad this way. It makes for great dipping and ease of eating. You can serve this to baby right off the spoon. For toddlers, tuna salad is fantastic to serve in lettuce cups, tomato or cucumber rounds, as a dip for homemade crackers or in a rice wrap.

notes: This salad also works well with canned salmon.

For yourself or for babies over 1 year, try adding ½ cup (46 g) crispy nuts. I love them in my tuna salad so I just add some into my serving separately. You can use almonds, pecans, walnuts—whatever you have! If you are on a nut-free diet, you can use any seeds such as pumpkin or sunflower.

chapter 8

mineral-rich side dishes

No boring vegetables here! The whole family can sit down to a meal and eat the same thing with these nourishing, simple sides that are also designed for babies 6 to 9 months and older (grain/nut/legume/egg white/sugar-free). The goal here is food that is delicious but not time-consuming to make, so these nourishing veggie sides can be at the dinner table every day of the week.

garlic-roasted red & golden beets

It is no secret how nourishing beets are, with their natural liver-cleansing properties and abundant vitamins and minerals. They were always really hard for me to "get down"... that is until I roasted them! And since garlic makes everything taste amazing, this very quick, colorful side dish is sure to please!

yield: 2 adult and 3 small-child servings

3 small red beets, peeled and diced

3 small golden beets, peeled and diced

3 tbsp (45 ml) melted butter

2 cloves of garlic, minced

1 tsp sea salt

¼ tsp ground pepper

Preheat the oven to 400°F (200°C).

Place the beets on a large baking sheet or jellyroll pan, toss the beets with the butter, garlic, salt and pepper and spread out on the pan evenly.

Roast the beets at 400°F (200°C) for 25 minutes until they are soft and slightly caramelized.

You can mash the beets with the back of a fork for baby, or pulse it with some bone broth. This makes great finger food for older babies and into toddlerhood!

note: To get fresh beets without a musty taste, I suggest buying them with the tops still on. The beets should feel hard. Cut the greens off when you get the beets home from the store. You can add beet greens to your bone broth, soups or smoothies, and they freeze well, too.

cinnamon sweet potato mash

Sweet potatoes make their way to our plates at least twice a week in some shape or form, and this is always a fun way to change things up. Sweet potatoes are loaded with vitamins and minerals and are energy powerhouses of slow-burning carbohydrates. This quick-cook method is super hands-free and great for busy nights!

yield: 2 adult and 3 small-child servings for 1–2 meals

3 medium sweet potatoes, coarsely cubed

3–4 tbsp (45–60 g) butter

½ tsp cinnamon

Sea salt and pepper to taste

Steam the sweet potatoes until they are fork-tender, about 20 minutes. If you do not have a steamer, you can boil the sweet potatoes until they are tender.

Put the cooked sweet potatoes, butter and cinnamon in your food processor and blend until the mixture is smooth. Add sea salt and pepper to taste and serve.

Baby can eat this right off the spoon with everyone else.

If there are leftovers that you don't want to use the next day, this dish freezes well.

notes: I like to serve this side with beef roast (page 123) and some greens.

Other warm spices—like cinnamon, nutmeg, ginger and cloves—work well with this too.

bacon sautéed green beans

This delicious side is a summer staple of ours when the garden is overflowing with green beans and we need a quick lunch!

yield: 2 adult and 3 small-child servings

3-4 strips of pastured bacon

½ lb (230 g) fresh or frozen (thawed) green beans

2 tbsp (6 g) fresh chopped chives

1 tbsp (4 g) fresh chopped parsley or 1-2 tsp (0.5-1 g) dried parsley

Sea salt and pepper to taste

Cook the bacon in a skillet over medium-high heat. Cook on each side for 1 to 3 minutes, depending on how thick the bacon is. Set aside, leaving the bacon grease in the pan for cooking additional ingredients. If there is a lot of grease, you can drain some of it. You will want about 2 tablespoons (30 ml) or so for cooking the green beans. You could use half bacon grease and half butter if you like that flavor as well.

Add the green beans to the skillet and cook on medium until they are bright green and tender. You can cook them about 5 minutes if you like a crisp "bite" to your green beans, or as long as 15 minutes if you like them softer.

Chop the cooked bacon. Then add the bacon, chives and parsley to the skillet to combine, and cook for 1 minute. Season with salt and pepper to taste.

Serve the green beans to baby cut up, finger-food style, making sure any of the bacon is in smaller bits and not too hard or crispy. You could puree the green beans and bacon with a little bone broth if you wish.

note: I like to cook the long string beans, but you can chop them before you cook them to make them easier for little ones to eat. Once my toddlers figured out how to take a bite from the long green beans, they always preferred them that way. If you have a little one who likes french fries, these can mimic the feel of them! And they are SO tasty!

garlic buttered "zoodles"

This is always a favorite with my kids. Who doesn't love buttery, cheesy noodles? Spiralizing zucchini performs noodle magic, and these really do feel like noodles! I love that zucchini has a rather mild flavor because you really can dress it up however you want.

When that summer zucchini is overflowing your garden or farmers' market, you can plan on this as a side dish with dinner weekly, or even add other chopped veggies to it and make it lunch!

yield: 2 adult and 3 small-child servings

---

3 tbsp (43 g) butter

2 large cloves of garlic, minced

2 medium zucchinis, spiralized

$\frac{1}{4}$ tsp sea salt

$\frac{1}{8}$ tsp ground pepper

Grated raw cheese or Parmesan

Melt the butter in a large skillet and add the garlic. Cook on medium-low heat for about 3 minutes.

Add the spiralized zucchini, salt and pepper, toss to combine (I like to use tongs), and turn the heat up to medium-high. The zucchini will release some water once the salt hits it, and you want to cook this off while the zucchini cooks. Cook for about 5 to 7 minutes until the zucchini "noodles" are cooked but still have a little bite to them.

Grate the cheese over each serving, or you can stir about $\frac{1}{3}$ cup (30 g) of grated cheese into the whole pan.

Baby can eat these zucchini noodles cut up on the plate as finger food or pureed with a little bone broth or water.

notes: Cut your "zoodles" before cooking them if they are really long. That will make it easier for the little ones to eat them.

Dress your "zoodles" up with fresh herbs of the season if you want! I like fresh basil or even a dried Italian herb blend.

herbed cauliflower "rice"

A fun way to get some extra vegetables on the plate, this delicious, buttery herbed cauliflower not only tastes good, but really does give the feel of having rice with your meal, especially when you still have babies eating at the table who cannot have grains yet.

While this makes a great dinner side, because the prep is so quick, I often serve it for lunch with butter or cheese and some soup.

yield: 2 adult and 3 small-child servings

1 small head cauliflower

¼ cup (57 g) friendly fat to cook in, such as butter, coconut oil, lard, tallow or avocado oil

¼ tsp sea salt

⅛ tsp ground pepper

2 tsp (6 g) fresh chopped thyme or ½ tsp dried thyme

2 tsp (6 g) fresh chopped oregano or ½ tsp dried oregano

Freshly grated raw cheese to garnish (optional)

Pulse the cauliflower in a food processor, or chop the cauliflower into rice-sized pieces.

Melt your friendly fat in a large skillet and add the riced cauliflower along with the salt, pepper and herbs. Cook on medium-high heat, keeping it moving, stirring here and there to keep it light and fluffy like rice. Cook the cauliflower around 5 to 6 minutes if you want a "bite" to it, or around 10 minutes if you want it softer.

Serve this to baby on the spoon or finger-food style. If baby is not yet handling small pieces of soft veggies, you could pulse it in the blender with a little bone broth or water.

notes: You can "rice" your cauliflower and keep it in the fridge, so this side dish can be even faster on a busy night.

You can substitute herbs that are in season where you live. I really like to use fresh dill in the summer. Sometimes in the winter I warm the flavors up with a curry blend.

maple-roasted acorn squash

Introducing kids to seasonal foods and the importance of eating with the seasons is a great goal that will reward you with kids who appreciate seasonal changes and harvest times, and have a better understanding of where their food comes from and how it grows. As the summer season changes to fall, we really look forward to enjoying fall and winter squashes again!

This maple-roasted squash will fill your home with an autumnal aroma that is really hard to resist! Kids eat this stuff up because it is sweet and delicious. This side dish is great because it can be served to baby right alongside the family at the dinner table.

Squash is a fantastic vegetable for the whole family, filled with vitamins and minerals, and it is easy to digest. Squash provides a steady, even carbohydrate energy source, and it tastes so good!

yield: 2 adult and 3 small-child servings

---

1 medium or 2 small acorn squashes, halved, with seeds scooped out

3 tbsp (43 g) butter

1–2 tbsp (15-30 ml) pure maple syrup

Sea salt and pepper to taste

Preheat the oven to 425°F (220°C).

Put the halved acorn squashes flesh-side up on a baking sheet, and butter the flesh.

Pour the pure maple syrup in the cavity of each squash half, and sprinkle with sea salt and pepper.

Roast at 425°F (220°C) for 50 to 60 minutes. The flesh of the squash should pierce easily with a fork and will have a caramelized look.

You can serve the squash as a side dish for the family, scooped right out of the shell, or, if you prefer a really smooth texture, you can scoop the roasted squash into a food processor or blender and puree. Babies new to squash will do best with the texture pureed, but you can definitely move to just scooping it out of the shell to their plate.

Leftovers can be kept in the fridge for about 5 days, or can be frozen for months in ice cube trays for baby servings or freezer-safe containers.

*See photo on page 126.

note: If you are serving the squash to babies between 5 to 9 months, the maple syrup is not necessary. The autumnal warmth it gives to this squash is fantastic, but those little ones don't really need the sweet addition to their squash. In the past, I have just left it out of the roasting method, and then added the maple to our plates individually, but omitted it from baby's.

pan-fried carrots & peas

This side dish was my answer to "What is the baby going to have for a veggie if we are having salads?" Especially in the summer, when we have salads as a family quite often, I needed a quick veggie side for the baby or toddler who couldn't chew a salad yet!

Not only are these peas and carrots really tasty, they are quick and easy finger foods! You can keep the leftovers in a container in the fridge as a quick pull-out snack that babies can feed themselves.

yield: 2 adult and 3 small-child servings

---

3 tbsp (43 g) friendly fat to cook in, such as butter, coconut oil, lard, tallow or avocado oil

3 large carrots, diced

1 cup (134 g) frozen peas, thawed

1 clove garlic, minced

¼ tsp sea salt

⅛ tsp ground pepper

Melt the friendly fat in a skillet and add the carrots and peas. Cook on medium heat until the carrots are tender, about 7 minutes.

Add the garlic and cook for a minute.

Serve the carrots and peas finger-food style, right on the plate. If baby isn't managing soft bits of veggies yet, you could puree them with bone broth or water.

note: Add fresh herbs if you have them around. I like tarragon with this.

butter-roasted potatoes with kale

Hesitant greens-eaters will fall in love with nutrient-rich kale when prepped with buttery, crispy potatoes! Chop the kale up small and they almost coat the potatoes like fresh herbs. The potatoes cook up crispy on the outside and creamy on the inside and it makes a really irresistible side dish to beef roast (page 123) or roasted chicken (page 116).

yield: 2 adult and 3 small-child servings

¼ cup (60 ml) melted friendly fat to roast with, such as butter, coconut oil, lard, tallow or avocado oil

4 medium russet potatoes, cubed

1 tsp onion powder

1 tsp garlic powder

½ tsp sea salt

¼ tsp ground pepper

½ lb (230 g) kale, de-ribbed and chopped

Preheat the oven to 425°F (220°C).

Toss everything together on a large sheet tray so the potatoes are evenly coated. Roast in the oven at 425°F (220°C) for 20 to 30 minutes until browned and crispy.

Serve to baby finger-food style right on the plate, or pulsed in a blender with a little bone broth or water.

parmesan-roasted broccoli florets

This is easily my girls' favorite side dish—as in all three of them! They can put away a pound of broccoli among them in one sitting, and that is all while arguing over who gets the last serving!

Broccoli is filled with vitamins and minerals that kids need, so tossing it with some yummy cheese and giving it that sweet, roasted feel is a great way to introduce this amazing vegetable to shy veggie eaters!

yield: 2 adult and 3 small-child servings

1 lb (450 g) fresh or frozen (and thawed) broccoli florets

3 tbsp (45 ml) melted friendly fat to roast in, such as butter, coconut oil, lard, tallow or avocado oil

2 cloves garlic, minced

¼–½ tsp sea salt

⅛ tsp ground pepper

¼ cup (25 g) freshly grated Parmesan

Preheat the oven to 425°F (220°C).

Put the broccoli florets on a baking sheet and toss with the friendly fat, garlic, salt and pepper, and roast in the oven at 425°F (220°C) for 20 minutes.

Take the roasted broccoli out, toss it with the Parmesan, and cook another few minutes to melt the cheese.

Serve the broccoli to baby cut up finger-food style right on the plate, or pureed with bone broth or water if baby isn't handling soft bits of veggies yet.

note: If you are using fresh broccoli, you can freeze the stalks to use in bone broth or to make my Simple Broccoli Soup (page 81).

garlic-roasted cabbage wedges

Cabbage is a year-round staple in our home, not only because it is delicious and easy to prepare, but also because it is really a frugal vegetable! Since we have cabbage, somehow, on the menu a couple times per week, I like to have a few different methods to prepare it so we can change things up.

This is a quick, hands-free method that lets me pop the dish in the oven while I'm busy with other things! Roasting cabbage gives it a mildly sweet flavor and it becomes nice and tender so little ones can manage it really well.

yield: 2 adult and 3 small-child servings

½ head cabbage, cored and sliced into wedges

¼ cup (60 ml) melted friendly fat to roast in, such as butter, coconut oil, lard, tallow or avocado oil

2 cloves garlic, minced

¼–½ tsp sea salt

⅛ tsp ground pepper

Preheat the oven to 425°F (220°C).

Lay the cabbage wedges flat on a baking sheet lined with a silicone baking mat or parchment paper, drizzle with friendly fat, rub the minced garlic over the tops and sprinkle with the salt and pepper.

Roast at 425°F (220°C) for 20 minutes until the cabbage wedges are tender and slightly browned or crisped along the edges.

Serve to baby cut up finger-food style right on the plate, or pureed with a little bone broth or water if baby is not ready for bits of soft veggies yet.

part 3

transitioning into toddlerhood

Building on the meals from Part 2, these nutrient-dense selections will help incorporate properly prepared, nourishing grains, nuts, legumes and egg whites for babies over the age of 1 year. We will also discuss how to handle holidays and special occasions with treats that are delicious but won't compromise on using real ingredients.

chapter 9

family breakfasts

Building on the nourishing breakfasts from Part 2, these delicious family breakfasts include properly prepared grains, nuts, legumes, and/or egg whites that toddlers over the age of 1 year can be introduced to when they are ready.

These breakfast bakes, muffins and quiches are some of my girls' favorite morning meals. Seeing those sweet smiles when they wake up to a warm breakfast is such a joy. Starting their day with a nutrient-dense meal sets the stage for a focused day of play!

nutrient-dense soaked oatmeal with fruit

Warm, comforting, creamy and delicious! Soaked porridges are a weekly staple in our breakfast rotation, and you can get so much nourishment in one bowl. Soaking the oats not only makes the grain easier to digest, it also makes it cook up quicker.

Note that this recipe will need to be planned in advance, allowing 8 to 12 hours for the oats to soak.

yield: 2 adult and 3 small-child servings

---

3 cups (240 g) old-fashioned oats or steel-cut oats (not quick oats)

Juice of 1 lemon for soaking

Water to cover oats, plus more for cooking if needed

3 tbsp (43 g) butter or coconut butter (see recipe for coconut butter page 189)

1½ cups (225 g) chopped fruit of choice

2 tsp (10 ml) vanilla or almond extract

Optional add-ins, such as unsweetened shredded coconut, crispy nuts or seeds, extra butter, raw cream, kefir or yogurt, and grass-fed collagen for protein and extra gut nourishment

Raw honey, blackstrap molasses or pure maple syrup to taste (optional)

Put the oats and lemon juice in a pot and cover the oats with water. Set the pot in a warm spot in your kitchen overnight for 8 to 12 hours. This soaking process breaks down the phytic acid in the grain so it can be digested more easily and helps the nutrients in the grain be absorbed better.

The next morning, add the butter, fruit, vanilla extract and any add-ins to the pot of soaked oats, and bring the oatmeal to a simmer for a few minutes to cook. You can cook it longer if you like thicker oatmeal, or add a little water if you like it thinner. Add your choice of sweetener if you need it, and serve.

notes: I would not add the extra sweetener for the younger toddlers. If they aren't used to sweeter tastes, don't fuss with their young palates; the fruit is sweet enough. You can add it to individual bowls if you wish.

Most weeks I make a double batch of just the plain oatmeal and keep it in the fridge. Then I can scoop out what I need on a busy morning and just warm through on the stove, add the fruit and be done!

You can put the add-ins into individual bowls too. My older girls like it when I have nuts, coconut, etc., sitting out in bowls for them to put in by themselves.

good morning breakfast bake

Everything you love about breakfast all in one dish! One of our weekend breakfast staples, this breakfast bake has become something I know like the back of my hand. I usually just get it all into the pan the night before and when I wake up I can pop it into the oven!

yield: 2 adult and 3 small-child servings

---

1 tbsp (14 g) butter

1 lb (450 g) pastured pork sausage, ham or bacon

1 medium onion, chopped

1 bell pepper, chopped

1-2 cups (91–182 g) chopped broccoli florets

3-4 cloves garlic, minced

2 tsp (2 g) dried thyme leaves

1 tsp sea salt

½ tsp ground pepper

8 pastured eggs

½-1 cup (45–90 g) organic cheese, shredded

2 cups (473 ml) whole sour cream

2-3 cups (120 g) day-old sourdough or gluten-free bread, chopped or broken up

Butter for greasing the pan

Warm a skillet over medium-high heat, melt the butter and crumble the sausage in. Cook the sausage over medium-high heat until it is cooked through and no longer pink, then set aside in a medium mixing bowl.

Using the sausage or bacon grease left in the skillet, cook the onion, bell pepper and broccoli with the seasonings until veggies are soft. You can add some butter if there isn't a lot of grease left in the pan. Add the cooked veggies to the bowl with the sausage.

In a separate bowl, beat the eggs, cheese and sour cream. Pour the egg mixture into the sausage and veggie mixture, and add the bread.

Pour the egg bake mixture into a buttered 9 x 13-inch (23 x 33-cm) pan and bake at 350°F (175°C) for 1 hour. Let it rest about 15 minutes before cutting.

notes: If you follow a grain-free diet or don't have bread around, use potatoes instead of bread and fry them up in the veggie-cooking step.

You can freeze squares of this bake for busy weekday morning breakfasts!

Change up the veggies to use what is in season! I love using slivered asparagus in the spring and adding tomatoes and zucchini in the summer. For the holidays, I use red and green bell peppers and serve it at our big family brunch! It serves a crowd wonderfully!

mini breakfast quiches

The perfect size for little hands, these mini breakfast quiches are my answer to weekend brunch! I like to sit with my coffee and breakfast and let the kids feed themselves. These little handheld quiches are the perfect portable, out-the-door breakfast for a busy school day as well with all of your favorite breakfast flavors.

yield: 12 mini quiches (muffin-sized)

---

1 tbsp (14 g) butter

1 lb (450 g) pastured ground sausage

1 cup (30 g) baby spinach or baby kale

Butter for greasing muffin tin

8 pastured eggs

3 tbsp (45 ml) whole raw milk or coconut milk

2 tbsp (30 ml) olive oil

$\frac{1}{2}$ tsp aluminum-free baking powder

1 tsp sea salt

$\frac{1}{4}$ tsp ground pepper

Freshly grated raw cheese for topping

Preheat the oven to 375°F (190°C).

Warm a skillet over medium-high heat, melt the butter in the skillet and crumble the sausage in. Cook the sausage over until it is cooked through and no longer pink, then set aside in a medium mixing bowl. Drain the grease, then combine the sausage with the spinach, off the heat.

Divide the sausage and spinach mixture into a 12-unit buttered muffin tin.

Whisk the eggs, milk, olive oil, baking powder, salt and pepper in a medium mixing bowl, and pour the egg mixture over the sausage and spinach mixture.

Top each quiche with cheese and bake in the oven at 375°F (190°C) for 20 to 25 minutes.

notes: You can freeze leftovers for quick on-the-go breakfasts. These keep well in the fridge for 3 days, or in the freezer up to 3 months.

Change up the veggies to what is in season! Slivered asparagus works really well as do bell peppers and zucchini.

cranberry walnut baked oatmeal

This warming breakfast tradition of our family is saved for "snow days." Warm and comforting, it is the perfect nourishing breakfast, topped with butter or cream, for cuddling up in heavy warm blankets and enjoying a fun snow day of fort making and coloring marathons!

Note that this recipe will need to be planned in advance, allowing 8 to 12 hours for the oats to soak.

yield: 2 adult and 3 small-child servings for 2 to 3 meals

for the oatmeal

2 cups (240 g) raw walnuts, finely chopped

4 cups (321 g) old-fashioned oats (not quick oats)

Juice of 1 lemon for soaking

2 tsp (10 g) sea salt

1 cup (93 g) unsweetened coconut shreds

2 eggs

2 cups (473 ml) unsweetened applesauce

$\frac{1}{3}$–$\frac{1}{2}$ cup (80–120 ml) pure maple syrup

$\frac{1}{3}$ cup (80 ml) melted butter or coconut oil

2 tsp (10 ml) almond extract

1$\frac{1}{2}$ cups (181 g) dried cranberries

Butter for greasing baking dish

for the topping

$\frac{1}{4}$ cup (57 g) butter

$\frac{1}{2}$ cup (62 g) flour of choice

$\frac{1}{2}$ cup (58 g) chopped crispy, toasted or raw walnuts

3 tbsp (45 ml) maple syrup

Put the walnuts, oats, lemon juice and sea salt in a large mixing bowl and fill with water to cover by an inch (2.5 cm). Give it a stir to combine and leave the bowl in a warm spot in your kitchen overnight (8 to 12 hours). This soaking process breaks down the phytic acid in the oats and nuts, making them easier to digest and making more of their nutrients available to be absorbed.

The next morning, put the oat mixture in a strainer to drain.

For the topping, in a small mixing bowl, combine into a crumble the butter, flour of choice, chopped walnuts and maple syrup.

Put the rest of the ingredients except the topping into the large mixing bowl, then combine it with the drained oat mixture.

Pour the batter into a buttered 9 x 13-inch (23 x 33-cm) baking dish, crumble the topping over it and bake uncovered at 375°F (190°C) for 1 hour. Let the baked oatmeal cool about 10 minutes before cutting.

notes: I like to freeze leftover squares for quick weekday breakfasts! If you want a smaller portion, simply halve the recipe and use a 9 x 9-inch (23 x 23-cm) square dish.

Coconut sugar or honey can be used in place of the maple syrup if you'd like. Also, vanilla extract would work instead of the almond extract, but if you have it, the almond flavor is so amazing in this!

fruit & honey sweetened soaked quinoa granola

Whether it is on those hot summer mornings where I don't want to warm the kitchen with cooking, or busy school mornings when we need to get out the door early, having a jar of homemade granola on hand is always very convenient. Simply sweetened with fruit and local honey, this delicious, quick breakfast is perfect swimming in a bowl of raw milk or coconut milk, or on top of a dish of yogurt. I also pack up granola for the school morning snack time for my younger ones.

Note that this recipe will need to be planned in advance, allowing 8 to 12 hours for the oats to soak.

yield: 2 adult and 3 small-child servings, plus extra for storage into 4 quart (4 L) jars

---

6 cups (482 g) old-fashioned oats (not quick oats)

2 cups (340 g) uncooked quinoa

2 cups (200–400 g) raw nuts such as pecans, almonds or walnuts, finely chopped or pulsed in the food processor

2 tsp (10 g) sea salt

Juice of 2 lemons

1 cup (112 g) coconut flour

½ cup (120 ml) melted friendly fat such as butter, coconut oil or avocado oil

⅓ cup (80 ml) raw honey

1 tbsp (15 ml) vanilla extract

5 cups (755 g) chopped seasonal fruit such as apples, strawberries, figs and pears

Put the oats, quinoa, chopped nuts, sea salt and lemon juice in a large mixing bowl. Add water to cover, combine and let the mixture soak 8 to 12 hours. This soaking process breaks down phytic acid in the grain, makes it easier to digest, and makes the nutrients more available to be absorbed.

After the grains and nuts have soaked, drain the liquid and return them to the mixing bowl. Add the rest of the ingredients and combine.

If you have a dehydrator, spread the granola onto your dehydrator trays and dehydrate at 135°F (60°C) overnight (or over the course of a day). I tend to soak the mixture during the day and dehydrate overnight. If you are using an oven, spread the granola on baking sheets, set your oven at the lowest heat (such as 150°F [65°C]) and stir throughout the day. Another option is to set the oven at a higher temperature, such as 300°F (150°C) or so, and bake the granola for about an hour, again stirring often until it is fully dried.

Once the granola is dried, you can crumble it into containers for storage. You can serve the granola with raw milk or coconut milk (see recipe for homemade coconut milk on page 62), or with whole yogurt. The texture is slightly crispy, but not too hard for toddlers to manage the chewing, though you can crumble the granola into smaller pieces for them if you wish. When my toddler is teething, I let the granola sit in the milk or yogurt for a bit to soak the liquid and get softer, and that works well too.

note: This granola is lightly sweetened. If you have older children who are used to sweeter cereal, you can bump the honey up a little or you can drizzle a little bit into their bowls.

soaked buckwheat pancakes with homemade berry syrup

Slightly sweet and nutty, these soft, delicious pancakes are a favorite Saturday morning breakfast in our house. Buckwheat is actually a seed and it is loaded with minerals that many of us are lacking, such as manganese, copper and magnesium. It is also a great source of fiber, so these pancakes won't leave the kids with a simple-sugar crash in an hour, especially when these pancakes are served with butter, a side of eggs or bacon and a glass of raw milk!

These pancakes are wholesome and delicious. You can make a fun weekend breakfast that everyone will love. The real berry syrup just puts it over the top, too!

Note that this recipe will need to be planned in advance, allowing 8 to 12 hours for the oats to soak.

yield: 2 adult and 3 small-child servings for 2 meals

2 cups (240 g) buckwheat flour

½ cup (79 g) brown rice flour

2 cups (475 ml) whole milk or coconut milk (see coconut milk recipe on page 62)

½ tsp sea salt

Juice of 2 lemons or 2 tbsp (30 ml) whole yogurt for soaking

2 eggs

½ cup (120 ml) avocado oil, melted butter or coconut oil

2–3 tbsp (30–45 ml) pure maple syrup or honey, plus more if needed

2 tsp (10 ml) almond extract

¾ cup (90 g) tapioca flour

1 tsp aluminum-free baking powder

½ tsp baking soda

2 cups (300 g) fresh or frozen berries of your choice, such as blueberries, strawberries or raspberries

2 tbsp (30 ml) water

Butter for cooking pancakes

Put the buckwheat flour, brown rice flour, milk, salt and lemon juice in a medium mixing bowl. Combine and let sit in a warm spot in your kitchen overnight, 8 to 12 hours. This soaking process reduces the phytic acid in the buckwheat seed, making it easy on digestion. It also allows the nutrients in the seeds to be absorbed easier.

After the soaking is done, in a separate small mixing bowl beat the eggs, avocado oil, syrup and almond extract until the mixture is fluffy, which takes about a minute, and then add this to the soaked buckwheat mixture.

Add the tapioca flour, baking powder and baking soda to the buckwheat mixture, and combine to make a smooth batter.

Heat your skillet or griddle to medium-high heat and melt a little butter in the pan. Spread ¼ cup (60 ml) of the pancake batter onto the hot griddle for each pancake. Cook for about 1 to 2 minutes. They will bubble in the middle when they are ready to flip. Flip and cook for an additional 30 seconds until golden on both sides, then set aside in a warm oven until ready to eat.

To make the fruit syrup, simply put the berries in a saucepan with the water and warm over medium heat. As the berries warm, you can squish them with the back of your wooden spoon. Bring the mixture to a medium simmer until the syrup thickens. You can serve this right over the pancakes as is, or put it in a blender to puree until smooth. If your berries are out of season and too tart, you can add a splash or two of raw honey or pure maple syrup.

note: If you tolerate gluten, you can use wheat flour instead of the brown rice flour if you wish.

chapter 10

family lunches & dinners

Building on the nourishing meals from Part 2, these delicious family meals include properly prepared grains, nuts, legumes and/or egg whites (as tolerated) that can be introduced to toddlers over the age of 1 year when they are ready to try them.

You can bring a special Asian "take out" night to your house or your favorite restaurant pasta dish right to your family table with nourishing ingredients! Bringing real-food meals to your home definitely doesn't mean boring. Make a spin-off of your favorite meals like winter hearty chili, made with real and nourishing ingredients.

sprouted white bean & garlic soup

Savory, creamy and warming, this comforting soup is made for those cool fall or bitter cold winter days. It uses the simplest of ingredients in the right way. You can enjoy a warm bowl of soup with the whole family and then pack up the leftovers in the work or school thermoses for the next day.

Note that this recipe will need to be planned in advance, allowing 8 hours for the beans to soak then 24 hours for them to sprout.

yield: 3½ to 4 quarts (3.5 to 4 L)

---

1 lb (450 g) organic dry white beans, such as cannellini or northern beans

¼ cup (57 g) friendly fat to cook in such as butter, tallow, lard, coconut oil or avocado oil

2 medium onions, coarsely chopped

Sea salt to taste

7 large cloves garlic, coarsely chopped

2½–3 quarts (2.5–3 L) bone broth, depending on how thick or thin you want the soup (see bone broth recipe on page 184)

1 tsp dried thyme leaves

1 tsp dried oregano

Pepper to taste

Put the dry beans in a large bowl, cover with about 3 inches (7.6 cm) of water and place the bowl in your oven (off, but with the light turned on) to soak for 8 hours. After the beans soak, drain them, rinse and then put them back into the bowl without water. Put them back under the light in your oven for about 24 hours to let them sprout a little. Rinse them a couple of times during this period. Putting them under the light in the oven will speed up the sprouting process, but if you live somewhere warm you might get away with putting them on your counter. This soaking and sprouting process breaks down the phytic acid in the beans, making them easier to digest as well as making their nutrients more available to be absorbed.

Melt the friendly fat in a large soup pot, add the onion with a big pinch of sea salt and cook for about 10 minutes over medium heat until they soften and sweeten.

Add the garlic and cook for a couple of minutes.

Add the broth and soaked/sprouted uncooked beans and bring to a boil with the lid on. Reduce to a high simmer and cook until the beans are tender, about 45 minutes. Check them around the 30-minute mark to see if the beans feel soft.

When the beans feel soft and cooked, add the thyme and oregano, and then blend with an immersion blender or in a regular blender until smooth. Season with sea salt and pepper to taste.

asian stir-fry with rice

It is really fun to have a "Chinese night" every once in a while on a Friday night! My husband and I often ate in Chinese restaurants while we were dating and the food has a lot of fond memories for me.

Traditional Asian cultures would have used fermented soy in their cooking, but that is not seen in many restaurants today. Synthetic, unfermented soy with an abundance of MSG is often used in Asian restaurants now, but that is just not a great idea to me, so we have given our modern Chinese dishes a real-food makeover using coconut aminos (which taste just like soy sauce) or the use of a truly fermented soy sauce which I have been able to find online.

yield: 2 adult and 3 small-child servings

for the breaded chicken

2 cups (250 g) cooked chicken, cubed (see roasted chicken recipe on page 116 or slow-cooker chicken recipe on page 36)

3 tbsp (28 g) white rice flour

3 tbsp (18 g) blanched almond flour

¼ cup (32 g) arrowroot flour

½ tsp red pepper flakes

½ tsp sea salt

¼ tsp pepper

1 tbsp (15 ml) coconut aminos

¼ cup (57 g) friendly fat to cook in, such as butter, tallow, lard, coconut oil or avocado oil

for the stir-fry

¼ cup (57 g) friendly fat to cook in, such as butter, coconut oil or lard

1 medium onion, sliced thin

6 cloves garlic, minced

4 cups (364 g) sugar snap peas or broccoli florets

1 tsp red pepper flakes, or more if you really like heat

4 medium to large carrots, cut with a julienne peeler to make strips of carrot

1 tbsp (15 ml) raw honey

⅓ cup (80 ml) coconut aminos

¼ cup (60 ml) water

½ tbsp (4 g) arrowroot powder

½ cup (95 g) long grain white rice or brown rice

(continued)

asian stir-fry with rice (cont.)

To bread the chicken, put the white rice flour, almond flour, arrowroot and seasoning in a bowl, pour the coconut aminos over the cooked chicken, and mix to moisten the chicken. Roll the chicken in the flour mixture to coat.

Put the coated chicken into a very hot large skillet or wok with the melted butter. Let the chicken brown well on all sides, letting it cook for a good couple of minutes on each. Take the chicken out of the pan to set aside while you make the rest of the stir-fry.

Add more fat to your pan or wok to melt, and add the onion with a big pinch of sea salt. Cook the onion over medium heat about 7 minutes until it is soft.

Add the garlic and cook for a minute.

Add the sugar peas and red pepper flakes and cook over medium heat for about 10 minutes. This will leave the peas with a little bite, which is how I like mine. If you want them softer, cook them for another 10 minutes. Add the julienned carrots and cook for a couple of minutes.

Put the honey, coconut aminos, water and arrowroot in a small bowl, whisk to combine, and then add this to the hot pan. Cook for a minute or two while the sauce thickens and then add the fried chicken that has been set aside earlier.

Make your ½ cup (95 g) of rice according to the instructions on your bag or box. The time will vary depending on whether you use a rice cooker, steamer or pot. Since I use a pot of water on the stovetop, I usually get my rice going before I even start making the stir-fry so it is done at the same time. If you choose to use brown rice, you will want to soak your rice overnight with water and an acid medium such as apple cider vinegar, yogurt or whey for better digestion.

note: If you tolerate gluten, you can substitute all sprouted wheat, such as Einkorn, for the chicken breading.

slow-cooker sprouted chili with vegetables

I grew up with a huge love for chili as we endure pretty long winters where I live. It reminds me of snowy, lazy, football-watching Sundays when I was a kid! There are many different approaches to chili, and while no one way is the right way, I think this is a happy medium of a really meaty chili and more of a soup/vegetable chili. There is a flavorful heat while still being family-friendly, so you can bump up the heat if your family enjoys that! I highly recommend increasing the smoky chipotle if that is the case. It really gives this chili a fantastic flavor that I just love.

Note that this recipe will need to be planned in advance, allowing 8 hours for the beans to soak, then 24 hours for them to sprout.

yield: 5 quarts (5 L)

---

1 lb (450 g) dried organic red or pinto beans

1 lb (450 g) grass-fed ground beef

2 medium onions, diced

3 zucchinis, chopped

3 green peppers, chopped

3 jalapeños, seeded, de-ribbed and diced

2 quarts (2 L) bone broth (recipe on page 184)

1 (15-oz [420-g]) can organic tomato sauce

2 (15-oz [420-g]) cans organic diced tomatoes

1½ tbsp (11 g) chili powder

1 tsp paprika

¼ tsp chipotle powder

1½ tbsp (22 g) sea salt, or less depending on how your bone broth is already seasoned

1 tbsp (15 ml) pure maple syrup

Whole sour cream or freshly grated raw cheese to garnish each bowl

To soak and sprout your beans for better digestion and nutrient availability, put the dry beans in a large bowl and fill with water to cover by about 3 inches (7.6 cm). Place the bowl in the oven (off, but with the light turned on) for 8 hours, and then drain. Put the beans back in your bowl without water and place under the light in your oven for about 24 hours. Rinse the beans a few times during the day and keep under the warm light. They will start to sprout within 24 hours.

Put the soaked and sprouted beans into the slow cooker along with the rest of the ingredients (except the sour cream and grated cheese) and cook on low 8 to 10 hours.

Garnish with sour cream or freshly grated cheese.

Freeze the leftovers for quick pull-out dinners. This one packs up well in thermoses to take to school or work.

notes: This recipe isn't overly spicy, but some kids can be sensitive to it. For little ones who have sensitive palates to "spicy" things, that whole sour cream really does the trick to tame the heat.

I like to soak my beans overnight. That way the next morning I can set the beans up to sprout over 24 hours, and the following morning, I can get the slow cooker going for the chili. The recipe is very hands-free once you get the hang of it! You can also soak and sprout the beans and then freeze them for quicker "dump it in" chili on a busy day.

You can double up the beef if you prefer a beefier chili.

veggie fried rice bowls

This is a quick weeknight one-pot meal that is full of delicious Asian flavor. Everything is the perfect little bite size for toddlers, and the next day I love to pack leftovers (if there are any!) into the school thermoses for the older kids!

yield: 2 adult and 3 small-child servings

---

1 cup (190 g) uncooked long grain white rice

2 tbsp (28 g) butter

3 pastured eggs, lightly beaten

3 tbsp (45 ml) sesame oil

3 carrots, diced

1 bunch green onions, sliced

2 tsp (4 g) freshly minced ginger, or 1 tsp dried/ground ginger

5 cloves garlic, minced

4 tbsp (60 ml) coconut aminos

3 tbsp (45 ml) organic white wine vinegar or rice vinegar

2 tbsp (30 ml) honey

1 big handful of baby spinach, chopped

Sea salt and pepper to taste

Cook the rice according to package instructions while you prepare the rest of the meal. If the rice is finished before you are done, just set it aside. Alternatively, you could use leftover rice from another meal or make the rice well beforehand.

Melt the butter in a large skillet and scramble the eggs. Put the scrambled eggs on a cutting board and chop to the size pieces you like in your fried rice. Set aside to add to the rest of the pan later.

Put the sesame oil in the skillet, and over medium heat cook the carrots for about 8 minutes until they are soft.

Add the green onions, ginger and garlic, and cook for a couple of minutes until the green onions are soft.

Add the coconut aminos, vinegar, honey, baby spinach and cooked rice, and cook until the spinach wilts and the liquid is absorbed. Add the cooked chopped egg, salt and pepper to taste, and serve. I like to use some fresh green onion to garnish the top.

note: I love the Asian flavor that the sesame oil gives this dish. But if you don't like sesame oil, you can cook in butter, lard, avocado oil or other friendly fats that won't change the flavor of the dish (i.e., coconut oil).

flavorful lentil soup

The humble lentil may be one of the most overlooked foods for a nourishing meal plan today. Not only can you make these neutral-flavored beans have any taste you want, but this is one of these ingredient staples that will make your real-food budget happier. Lentils are a great source of protein, fiber and minerals and can make a great, budget-friendly lunch or simple supper.

Note that this recipe will need to be planned in advance, allowing 8 hours for the beans to soak, then 24 hours for them to sprout.

yield: 6 quarts (6 L)

---

1 lb (450 g) dried organic lentil beans

¼ cup (57 g) friendly fat, such as butter, coconut oil, tallow or lard

3 medium onions, chopped

3 carrots, chopped

3 celery stalks, chopped

Sea salt to taste

7 cloves garlic, minced

1 (28-oz [784-g]) can organic diced tomatoes, drained

2 quarts (2 L) bone broth

½ tsp dried basil

½ tsp thyme

¼ tsp cumin

¼ tsp marjoram

Pinch of cayenne pepper

Pepper to taste

To soak and sprout your beans for better digestion and nutrient availability, put the dry lentils in a large bowl with water to cover by about 3 inches (7.6 cm). Place the bowl in the oven (off, but with the light turned on) for 8 hours, and then drain. Put the drained beans back in the bowl and place under the light in your oven for about 24 hours. Rinse the beans a few times during the day and keep under the warm light. They will start to sprout within 24 hours.

In a large stockpot, cook the onion, carrot and celery in the friendly fat with a few pinches of sea salt to bring out their juices and sweeten and soften. Cook over medium to medium-high heat for about 10 minutes, and then add the garlic and cook for a minute.

Add the soaked/sprouted beans, diced tomatoes, broth and seasonings, bring to a boil and then reduce to a simmer with the lid on. Cook for around 30 minutes until the beans are bite-tender.

Take out about half of the soup and puree with an immersion blender, or in a regular blender, and then return the puree to the soup. This will give the soup a beautiful creaminess. If you like the soup thinner, you can skip this step entirely.

Pack up leftovers into the freezer for quick pull-out lunches or dinners. This is also a great thermos soup for school or work.

note: I like to soak my beans for this soup during the day, setting them up first thing in the morning. That way, they are finished soaking by mid-afternoon, they can sprout over 24 hours, and the next afternoon I can get the soup made for dinner. The recipe is very hands-free, once you get the hang of it! You can also soak/sprout your beans and then freeze them for quicker "dump it in" soup-making on a busy night.

restaurant-style chicken, veggies & pasta with a garlic cream sauce

This is my go-to meal for special birthday dinners at home, or just a Friday night when I want to feel like we actually have a babysitter and can go out on a date!

This dish will taste and feel like you have been in the kitchen all day, but this dinner can be made in just 30 minutes! With creamy garlic sauce, vegetables, chicken and decadent pasta, this dish is the perfect end to a busy week, and will bring everyone around the table to share a meal.

yield: 6 quarts (6 L), serves 2 adults and 3 small children

½ lb (230 g) pasta, preferably a sprouted variety or a gluten-free rice noodle

3 tbsp (43 g) friendly fat, such as butter, coconut oil, tallow, lard or avocado oil

1 small onion, diced

½ lb (230 g) mushrooms, sliced

Sea salt to taste

5 cloves garlic, minced

1½ cups (360 ml) white wine of choice

½ lb (230 g) fresh or frozen (thawed) broccoli florets, sliced lengthwise

1½ cups (225 g) fresh or frozen (thawed) peas

2 cups (250 g) cherry tomatoes, halved

2-3 cups (250-375 g) cooked chicken, chopped (see roasted chicken recipe on page 116 or slow cooker chicken recipe on page 36)

1-1½ cups (240-360 ml) raw milk, cream or coconut milk or a combination (see coconut milk recipe on page 62)

Pepper to taste

Freshly grated Parmesan or other raw cheese to garnish (optional)

Cook the pasta until it is par-cooked, not quite al dente. It will cook the rest of the way in the cream sauce and thicken it with its starches.

While the pasta is cooking, melt the friendly fat in a large and deep skillet, add the onion and mushrooms with a big pinch of sea salt and cook on medium heat for about 10 minutes until the vegetables are softened and slightly caramelized.

Add the garlic and cook for a minute, and then add the wine to de-glaze the pan.

Bring the wine to a simmer and then add the broccoli, peas and tomatoes and cook over medium-high heat for about 7 minutes until the broccoli is bite-tender and bright green.

Add the cooked chicken, milk and the par-cooked pasta, bring to a simmer and cook until the pasta is al dente and the starches from the pasta have thickened the cream sauce. Season with sea salt and pepper to taste and garnish each plate with freshly grated Parmesan or other raw cheese if you wish.

notes: The wine gives a depth of flavor that I really love and the alcohol is cooked off. If you prefer, you can use bone broth instead.

This makes enough to feed my family of five for one meal. You can adjust the recipe as needed for larger or smaller portions.

Change up the vegetables to what is in season. My 5-year-old loves this made with spring asparagus for her springtime birthday!

chapter 11

occasional treats

From first birthdays to family holidays, yes it is okay for toddlers to celebrate, too! Food was meant to be enjoyed, and real food tastes pretty amazing! These recipes are appropriate for babies aged 1 and older on a very occasional basis, allowing us to celebrate those special occasions with a special treat!

Note that all of these special, occasional treats are sweetened with unrefined sugar. Whether you use raw honey or pure maple syrup, you really can make treats without processed sugar! You can substitute organic pure cane sugar or coconut sugar for all of these recipes if you wish, and when my budget doesn't allow for the use of all that raw honey, that is what I use, too. Whole cane sugar (for example, Sucanat brand) is another great natural sweetener; just note that it does change the color of whatever you are adding it to.

nourishing raw cocoa avocado pudding

Rich and creamy chocolate pudding with a nourishing kick! Because this delicious pudding is mostly avocados, I make it every so often as an after school snack, too!

yield: 2 adult and 3 small-child servings

---

3 ripe avocados, pitted and scooped out of the shell

1 tsp vanilla extract

$\frac{1}{4}$–$\frac{1}{3}$ cup (60–80 ml) raw honey

6 tbsp (42 g) raw cacao or carob

Pinch of sea salt to garnish

Put everything, except the salt, into your food processor and blend until smooth. Serve each bowl with a pinch of coarse sea salt if you wish.

nutrient-dense vanilla bean pudding

Real pudding is actually loaded with nutrients from whole milk and pastured yolks, so while this sweet treat is still just something we have on occasion, it is definitely one you can feel good about! It is rich and creamy, and the flavor is warm and delicious.

yield: 2 adult and 3 small-child servings

1½ cups (360 ml) whole milk or coconut milk (see coconut milk recipe on page 62)

2 egg yolks

⅓ cup (80 ml) natural sweetener of choice (I like to combine raw honey and pure maple syrup)

3 tbsp (42 g) tapioca starch or arrowroot starch

3 tbsp (43 g) butter

1 vanilla bean, scraped, or 1 tsp vanilla extract

1 tsp almond extract

Beat the milk and yolks in a small mixing bowl and pour into a small saucepan.

Add the rest of the ingredients to the saucepan.

Turn the heat on to medium or medium-high and whisk until the mixture begins to gather bubbles at the edges. Keep the heat at medium for about 8 to 10 minutes, whisking almost constantly so the bottom doesn't stick or scorch.

After you cook the pudding for about 8 to 10 minutes, it will be slightly less thick than pudding but will thicken the rest of the way in the fridge. Pour the cooked pudding into a medium bowl, or smaller serving bowls, and refrigerate. The pudding will take a few hours to thicken and cool completely. The pudding will keep for 2 to 3 days in the refrigerator.

how to make a fruit sorbet with any fruit

One of my biggest summer delights is picking fruit with the girls and then making something fun with it after all of the hard work of picking, washing and storing. Simply adding some honey and milk to the fruit and using the ice cream maker makes for a fun, seasonal treat without refined sugar, and gives the kids a love for real ingredients.

If there are farms nearby where you can pick your own fruit, give it a try! It will give the kids an appreciation for where this special treat comes from. Also check your local farmers' markets or local fruit stands for delicious fresh fruit. Frozen fruit can be used if fresh is not available.

yield: 1½ quarts (1.5 L)

---

4 cups (600 g) fresh or frozen (thawed) fruit such as strawberries, cherries, pineapple or peaches

⅓ cup (80 ml) raw honey

1½ cups (360 ml) whole raw milk

Juice of 1 lemon

1½ tsp (7 ml) vanilla or almond extract, depending on the fruit you are using

Put the fruit in a medium saucepan and bring to a simmer. Smash the fruit as it cooks (I like to use a potato masher) and simmer for 10 minutes.

Put the cooked fruit into a blender or food processor, add the honey and puree completely.

Add the rest of the ingredients, combine and then set the sorbet mixture in the fridge to chill for an hour.

After the sorbet mixture chills, give it a quick stir, add it to your ice cream machine, and process in the ice cream machine according to the manufacturer's instructions. The ice cream will finish with a texture of a really soft soft serve but will harden more in the freezer. It will take about 6 to 12 hours to harden.

notes: If raw milk is not available, try to avoid ultra-pasteurized, or use coconut milk instead.

Some of our favorite flavors are cherry almond (with almond extract), peaches and cream (using vanilla extract), tropical coconut with pineapple and coconut milk, strawberry vanilla and raspberry almond.

vanilla bean ice cream with berry sauce topping

Vanilla just happens to be my very favorite flavor for desserts of any shape and kind, so I have a real love and appreciation for using real vanilla beans in my cooking. There really isn't anything quite like it, and while a good vanilla extract definitely still does the trick, there is just something about having that vanilla bean swirled through your ice cream that puts it over the top in amazing flavor.

This ice cream is every bit as creamy and delicious as your favorite ice cream stand or store brand with all nourishing, real ingredients! It is a family favorite topped with the kid's choice of berry sauce flavor for topping!

yield: 2 quarts (2 L)

for the vanilla ice cream

3 cups (700 ml) whole organic cream, preferably raw

¼ cup (60 ml) pure maple syrup

3 pastured egg yolks

2 scraped vanilla beans plus 2 tsp (10 ml) vanilla extract, or 1 tbsp (15 ml) vanilla extract total

½ tsp sea salt

for the berry sauce topping

2 cups (300 g) organic berries, fresh or frozen

2-4 tbsp (30-60 ml) raw honey, depending on how sweet you want the sauce

To make the ice cream, put all of the ice cream ingredients into a large mixing bowl, blend well with hand beaters to combine and set the ice cream mixture into the fridge for an hour to chill.

After the ice cream chills, stir it through one more time, put it into your ice cream maker and process according to the manufacturer's instructions. The ice cream will resemble soft serve when it comes out of the ice cream maker, and you can transfer the finished ice cream to the freezer to harden further (it takes about 6 or so hours to harden to the texture of ice cream) or you can serve it as is.

To make the berry sauce topping, warm the berries over medium to high heat until the berries soften and release their juices. I like to use a potato masher to mash them as I go. Let the berries slow simmer for about 10 minutes, turn the heat off and then add the honey. The sauce will thicken on its own. You can blend the sauce completely if you don't like bits of fruit in your topping.

notes: The berry sauce topping works with cherries or peaches, too!

You can replace the cream with whole coconut milk if your diet is dairy-free or you don't have access to quality dairy.

You can substitute 3 tablespoons (23 g) of tapioca flour for the eggs if you cannot have eggs or do not have access to quality pastured eggs. Since this recipe uses raw egg yolk, I would recommend only using pastured eggs.

You can add a tablespoon (15 ml) of organic vodka to the ice cream mixture to keep the ice cream from hardening completely. (The alcohol helps prevent this.)

how to make whipped cream topping for any dessert

Fluffy, creamy whipped topping is just minutes away! Show the kids how real whipped cream is made, and make a refined-sugar-free delicious whipped topping for any dessert. Not only does homemade whipped cream taste amazing, it is also so easy!

yield: 1 quart (1 L)

1 pint (475 ml) organic whole cream, preferably raw

3 tbsp (45 ml) pure maple syrup or raw honey

1 tsp vanilla or almond extract (depending on what flavor the dessert is)

Put everything into a medium mixing bowl and beat with a whisk attachment for 2 to 3 minutes until the cream is fluffy.

notes: This can be made ahead of time but it does deflate after about a day. Simply beat again with the whisk to fluff it back up.

This recipe works for coconut cream as well! Put your coconut milk (page 62) in the fridge and then pull the cream off the top to use for the cream.

I really love to use real vanilla bean for my whipped cream. The little flecks of vanilla bean are just icing on the cake for me, but if you prefer a more traditional-looking whipped cream just stick with the extract.

buttered raw cacao hot cocoa

Our favorite winter holiday treat, this rich and creamy hot cocoa made with raw cacao is perfect for sitting next to a warm fire, piling on the heavy blankets and reading books, and warming up with after hours of playing in the snow!

yield: 2 mugs

2 cups (475 ml) raw milk or coconut milk

3 tbsp (21 g) raw cacao powder

2 tbsp (30 ml) raw honey

1 tbsp (15 g) butter

1 tsp vanilla extract

½ tsp peppermint extract (optional)

Slowly warm the milk in a small saucepan over medium heat. If you heat the milk too fast, you will scorch it and it will not taste good. You can also maintain a lot of the raw milk properties if you keep the temperature below 118°F (48°C).

Put the warm milk and the rest of the ingredients into a blender and blend until smooth. Serve warm as is or top with homemade whipped cream.

notes: This makes two adult-sized mugs. I usually split one mug with my 6-year-old and 4-year-old to help with serving sizes. Older children will probably enjoy a full mug. Younger toddlers between 2 and 3 years old probably only need a quarter to a half mug.

You can add a candy cane as special treat. There are so many options for candy canes made with natural dyes available now in stores and online.

part 4

traditional staples

These are the nutrient-dense building blocks to structure your daily meals around. Included here are tips on how to fit in the routine of making these staples, even with a busy schedule. These important diet components will not only nourish your family, but will give your baby a solid, nutrient-dense start while his or her brain, digestive system and whole body are in critical development stages.

how to make nourishing slow-cooker bone broth

If there is one traditional food that I usually recommend as a first step to making nourishing food in the home, it is bone broth. Traditional cultures knew what they were doing keeping this nourishing staple at the core of most of their cooking.

Not only is there less waste when we use every part of the animal, but hidden in those bones are vital minerals and vitamins that our bodies are so desperately craving to function, as well as gelatin to make for a sound digestive system. This is one of the single most cost-effective and frugal ways to bring nutrient-loaded food to your family's meals.

Make your bone broth from the bones of healthy animals that are available where you live. Where I live, healthy pastured chickens, grass-fed cattle and wild-caught fish are the most abundant. I live in the Midwest, where many people also do a lot of wild game hunting, so venison broths are popular among hunting families and are just delicious.

Use your bone broth for bases for soups and stews, cooking reductions and sauces, and also drink it straight from the mug! I use a small spoon or medicine syringe to introduce bone broth to my babies from about 5 months old. When they are older, it is so nice to give them a mug of warm bone broth when they feel ill and know that they will happily drink it!

yield: 3 quarts (3 L)

Bones from a chicken, cow, fish or other healthy animal enough to fill your slow cooker at least ¼ to ½ of the way up

3 carrots, coarsely chopped

3 stalks of celery , coarsely chopped

1 medium onion, coarsely chopped

4 cloves garlic, coarsely chopped

2 tbsp (30 ml) apple cider vinegar

Sea salt, pepper and other seasonings as needed

Filtered water to fill the slow cooker to the top

Put the bones, veggies and vinegar into the slow cooker and fill it to the top with cold water. Let the mixture sit without the heat on for 30 to 60 minutes to allow the apple cider vinegar to draw the minerals from the bones.

Turn the slow cooker on low for 24 hours. After 24 hours, strain your broth. Season with sea salt, pepper and other seasonings as you use it in various different recipes. You can store your bone broth in the fridge for a week or in the freezer for months.

(continued)

how to make nourishing slow-cooker bone broth (cont.)

My biggest tip for busy families is to just figure out what works for you. I have been through seasons of life where it is easiest for me to get my huge oven roaster out and do a really large load of bones to make gallons of bone broth at a time to freeze and store away. And yet there are other seasons of life I find it simpler to just make a slow cooker of bone broth once a week with the whole chicken we cook. Just find a rhythm that works with your family's flow and it won't feel like something that is taking up too much of your time. My last piece of advice is to enjoy it. In my experience, there is a huge satisfaction that comes with this simple task of making broth. It pulls you back to your traditional roots, no matter how modern this world has become.

notes: If the bones are uncooked, you will want to roast them first for better flavor. (For instance I get bags of the bones from the cow we purchase and they are uncooked.) Just set the bones on a baking sheet in an oven at 400°F (200°C) for about an hour. Specifically, with larger marrow bones like that from a cow, you can scrape the marrow out after cooking, to eat or freeze for another soup or stew addition. My kids love it spread on homemade crackers. I also save the fat that runs off from the bones. You can use it for cooking and it is just delicious.

If you are using chicken, ask your chicken farmer for the feet. This adds a tremendous amount of gut-healing gelatin to the bone broth.

I keep a bag of veggie scraps in my freezer to add to my broths so I rarely have to add all "new" vegetables to make broth, everything from kale ribs to carrot tops, celery leaves to those little pieces of garlic in the middle of the garlic bulb that no one wants to peel! I even like to add some nettles to my bone broth for extra minerals.

how to render grass-fed tallow or pastured lard in the slow cooker

It's no secret that traditional fats like tallow and lard are making a comeback from the days when they were thought of as evil foods that clogged our arteries. In fact, grass-fed tallow and lard are much easier to find these days and are even being sold commercially!

Tallow and lard have a permanent spot in my cooking fat arsenal not only because they have a neutral flavor and withstand heat very well in keeping their structure, but also because of their nutrient properties. Lard from pigs on pasture has one of the highest vitamin D contents of any food. (Tallow is a good source of vitamin D as well.) The friendly saturated fat in tallow and lard is extremely important for growth, development, hormone production and organ functioning. It also provides a satiating factor to meals, stabilizing blood sugars.

It is really easy and cost-effective to render your own tallow or lard, so if you have a local source it is a great frugal way to go, and you can support a local farmer too!

yield: about 2–3 quarts (2–3 L), depending on the animal

4–5 lbs (1.8–2.2 kg) grass-fed beef or lamb fat (called suet) or pastured pig fat (called leaf lard)

About ½ cup (120 ml) water per pound (450 g) of fat

Cut the fat into pieces that are manageable for your food processor, and then use your food processor to pulse the fat into small pea-sized pieces.

Put the fat into a large slow cooker, add the water, and cook on low for 1½ to 2 hours.

Strain out the pieces that are left (you can discard or feed to your pets!), and store the rendered fat in the fridge for 3 to 6 months. You can freeze the rendered fat in the portion sizes you want and it will last longer.

notes: The tallow will be yellow when you strain it and will become cream or white in color as it cools and is refrigerated. Shelf life in the fridge is a good 3 to 6 months! I store a cup or two in the fridge and the rest I store in half-cup portions in the freezer for months.

Rendered lard makes the best pie crusts! Both tallow and lard are not only great for any cooking, but they are excellent for frying. You can cook some potato rounds in your tallow and make the best potato chips you have ever tasted!

how to make coconut butter

Coconut butter is a fun, easy and gentle first food for baby that will transition into toddlerhood and childhood diets as a favorite topping for sourdough toast or as a nourishing add-in stirred into their breakfast oatmeal. I like to introduce coconut butter right off the spoon as a first food. Baby will love the mild sweetness and creamy, easy-to-manage texture. To this day, my older girls think of it as "frosting" when I spread it over pancakes or crackers!

Coconut butter is essentially the "meat" of a coconut blended until creamy. It has every part of the coconut in addition to the oil. So the meaty fiber with all of the benefits of the oil, such as lauric acid like that found in breast milk, and friendly saturated fat are all contained in one delicious spoonful. While you can certainly find coconut butter to buy just about anywhere these days, it is super easy to make on your own and more cost-effective.

yield: about 1 ½ to 1 ¾ cups (344–402 g) coconut butter

---

2 cups (151 g) unsweetened, finely shredded coconut

Put the coconut in your food processor or high-powered blender and blend until the coconut is creamy, scraping the sides down frequently. The whole process takes a good 15 to 20 minutes, start to finish, for the food processor, and a little less with a high-powered blender. Store your coconut butter at room temperature or in the fridge. Note that it will harden in the fridge, but it is easily melted on the stove or by putting the jar of coconut butter in a bowl of hot water.

note: I get shredded coconut in bulk at our local health food store. You can find it pretty much anywhere these days, including popular online sites.

how to give cod-liver oil to a baby

One of the very first foods you can introduce to your baby to promote a strong immune system and robust cognition is cod-liver oil. Particularly in babies and children whose brains are growing very rapidly, the EPA and DHA fatty acids in cod-liver oil are extremely important to nourish the neurons. Cod-liver oil is also naturally, perfectly designed with the right ratios of vitamin A to D which is critical for the immune health as well, and the fatty acids in the oil help these fat-soluble vitamins to be absorbed by the body.

You can start offering tastes of cod liver oil when the baby is as young as 3 or 4 months old. I start with just a little drop on a small spoon into their mouth. You can use a medicine syringe if you wish. I didn't start my first born on cod-liver oil until she was closer to age 1 and she really fought it. It is really much easier to introduce baby to it early and develop their taste for it. My children, now at ages 7, 5 and 3, take cod-liver oil every single morning without batting an eye. My first born, who as a baby didn't take to it right away, now sometimes reminds me that we need to take it!

If you have older toddlers or children who have not yet tried cod-liver oil, my recommendation would be to first of all not make a huge deal out of it. Don't tell them it might taste bad. To be honest, many of them might take right to it without a fuss, especially if you are using a clean, extra virgin brand that doesn't taste super fishy. Just do a half dose to start so there isn't as much in their mouths and you can have a glass of water or raw milk nearby, if that helps to chase it down. I still haven't gotten used to the feel of it in my mouth. It is a texture thing with me, but I didn't start taking cod-liver oil until adulthood. You can talk with them, too, in age-appropriate ways, about the benefits of cod-liver oil! My oldest will tell you how it is a "super" food and helps her brain grow and keeps her body healthy. My youngest will tell you how it makes her grow big and strong. You can choose to word it as you wish but that gives you an idea!

I follow the Weston A. Price Foundation dosing recommendations of children ages 3 months to 12 years old, ¼ to ½ teaspoon, and children over 12 years old and adults, ½ to 1 teaspoon.

a list of "friendly fats" to use in food prep & cooking
why children need them, and which ones are safe

It may be in the back of the book, but this very well may be my favorite section! I am so passionate about teaching people how vital friendly fats are to children. I spent so many years of my childhood, teens and early 20-somethings with a brain and endocrine system literally starved of fat. I grew up right in the middle of the "low fat" fad, and it truly robbed an entire generation of the very substance that makes hormones, metabolism and growth actually work.

Animal fats like tallow, lard and even butter have such amazing health benefits for teens and adults, too. Not only do they make food taste good, but they really can make positive health changes in your body, from lowering cholesterol to burning unwanted body fat using naturally derived conjugated linoleic acid (CLA), and helping stabilize blood sugar.

So go ahead and spread that butter over your veggies! Not only will the kids gladly eat them that way, but the vitamins in those veggies are fat-soluble… meaning they need some fat to absorb into your tissues!

It is best to avoid transfats and industrialized oils like canola, soy, corn, safflower and cottonseed oils, especially in growing children, so here is a list of safe, friendly fats for your family.

safe, friendly fats to include in food prep and cooking

Butter

Beef or lamb suet or tallow

Pig lard

Chicken fat

Goose or duck fat

Organic cold-pressed coconut or palm oil

Avocado oil

Extra virgin olive oil

Expeller-pressed sesame oil

sourcing tips

Animal-based fats are best sourced from local farmers to ensure grass-fed or pasture raising. There are some reliable animal-based grass-fed fats you can find online with a quick Google search. The coconut, palm, avocado, olive and sesame oils can be found sourced organically at even mainstream grocery stores, though certainly health food stores will carry them, too. I like to use Costco to save on our budget so if you have one near, that is an option. You can also find all of them online through Amazon or other online shopping options.

a list of important probiotic rich fermented foods to include

Traditional cultures very often preserved their food using a variety of fermenting methods. Culturing vegetables and other foods such as raw milk for kefir and yogurt provide loads of beneficial bacteria, enzymes, vitamins and minerals to our bodies.

Not only are fermented foods very nourishing, they are also easy for kids to eat and gentle on digestion! I was always very surprised at how well all three of my kids took to soured foods, almost as if they were innately designed to take them in. It took my adult palate, that had never had real fermented foods in my life, a while to get used to them, but they make their way to our table daily now and I quite enjoy it!

This book will not cover specific recipes for fermenting a variety of foods, as that would take an entire book itself because there are so many possible recipes! Instead, use this list as inspiration to add to your baby's and family's diets. There are so many fermented food recipes at the library, bookstores and online! Have fun with it! Those wanting to start out slow and ease into things may want to look for pickles and sauerkraut that are commercially sold and traditionally fermented. Check out your local farmers' markets and local health food stores. You just might be surprised at what you find! I purchase one of the best kimchis (spicy fermented cabbage) I have ever tasted from a local company.

fermented food ideas for the family

Fermented vegetables of any kind are delicious and easy to buy or make from scratch, from dilly beans and carrots to sauerkraut and pickles! My babies literally would grab the sauerkraut jar out of my hands for more! They love this stuff. And you don't need anything more than a jar, some cabbage and a little sea salt. Fermented vegetables are super easy!

Fermented dairy from raw cow or goat milk such as kefir, yogurt, sour cream, cheese and cream cheese are big hits with kids too. You will need a starter culture from a place such as Cultures for Health online to make these, though ask around at farmers' markets and real-food groups like Weston Price chapters in your area, and there just may be someone willing to share a starter culture with you!

Other fermented drinks such as water kefir and kombucha can be great alternatives to those sensitive to dairy and are super easy to make. You will need a starter culture for these as well . You can use places such as Cultures for Health online or ask around for a culture someone might be willing to share.

notes about organic vs. conventional

Shopping for organics versus non-organics is a question that comes up a lot. Everyone comes from different parts of the world where certain things are available or not. Everyone comes from different financial places in life. And everyone comes from different viewpoints on things. Because I understand all of this, note that this is my approach to organics versus conventional food and you need to do what works for you and your family. For instance, ingredient lists in the book do not always say organic next to produce items because I don't want you to pass by a recipe and not make it just because you can't find or afford an organic carrot. I would much rather you make that homemade meal for your family using conventional food than go to a fast food restaurant or buy a processed meal!

When it comes to fruits and vegetables I shop the "Dirty Dozen" and "Clean 15." These two lists are published by the Environmental Working Group (EWG), and every year they update the lists naming common fruits and vegetables containing the most and least pesticides. You can find the most updated EWG lists at http://www.ewg.org. Because my household budget does not allow me to buy organic for every single produce item, and because not every single produce item is offered organically where I live, this has been my happy medium to ensuring we are avoiding foods that are heavily laden with pesticides, but also so we are able to get a variety of fruits and vegetables in every single day. We take advantage of local U-picks and preserve or freeze as much as we can to save money, and shop locally when we can. I shop around. If the local asparagus is $5 per pound at the farmers' market but $2 or $3 per pound at our local grocer (and usually still from the region) then I have to take that lower cost every time, based on our family budget. I support local all I can and the rest of the time we have to do what we have to do. Don't go broke trying to eat healthy. It isn't worth it. We have been there!

My biggest non-compromise financially in my house is animal products. Anything meat, milk, eggs, cheese is going to be pasture-raised/grass-fed, non-hormone and antibiotics, and non-GMO as much as possible. We live in an area where these items are pretty abundant, and while they are pricier than store bought, it is still very do-able financially for us. This is not the case in every part of the country or in every part of the world, however! I literally have friends in some areas of the country who have zero grass-fed farms or options within 2 or 3 hours of them, and others who can easily go to the store and pick up a carton of raw grass-fed milk.

Do your research, shop around, check local Weston Price chapters, and search online through places like the Eat Wild website. You might be surprised at what you find! Also don't underestimate what you might find at places like your local grocer or larger chains and big-box discount stores, like Costco. Our regular local grocer (not a health food store) carries a brand of pastured eggs with no hormones or antibiotics, as well as a variety of organic produce and organic pantry items. Some big-box discount stores carry a very large variety of real-food items like coconut oil, and while the produce may not always be local, much of it is frozen organic and great quality.

acknowledgments

In my wildest dreams I don't think I ever would have pictured myself writing a book. Writing was a "hobby" I took up to maintain my sense of humanity in the midst of the fogginess of newborn-hood. Motherhood had a way of fueling the fervor in me to see kids grow up loving real food, because I was seeing with my own two eyes that it truly was possible, and a passionate writer was born.

Interestingly enough, this has been the hardest part of the book for me to write. There are so many people involved in putting a book together, and I never realized what goes on the behind the scenes until actually doing it myself. I have had the vision for this book in my head for over 3 years, and there are so many people along the way that have had their hand in the making of this book.

I remember the torn feeling of getting a book offer and wondering how in the world would I ever have the time to do this with 3 small children at home. Without hesitation, my husband said, "Because I can help, and people need the book you are going to write." Christopher, thank you for being my rock and helping me figure out how to fit writing a book into our family's schedule without disrupting our kids. You have been my #1 supporter from day one, believing in me right from the very first blog post I wrote, and I cannot imagine doing this without you by my side. Thank you for letting me mess up our kitchen with test recipes, and then, without asking, helping me clean it up. Thank you for taking on the grocery shopping, homework, laundry and meal making on the days book writing encompassed my every minute. I love you more than words can say.

Chloe, Claire and Caitlyn, you, my sweet girls, were at the forefront of my mind with every word I wrote in this book. You are the purpose behind this passion, and I am so proud of each of you. You are my favorite recipe testers; with every "mmm" and devoured plate, you are my biggest encouragement.

To my publisher and editor, Will and Sarah, at Page Street Publishing, thank you for believing in such a new writer and in my message. Thank you for listening to my every (picky!) detailed vision for this book and running with them. I appreciate the opportunity you have given my family to see this project through.

I am so thankful to the seasoned writers and my mentors who have given me a chance to write for them on their blogs, believing in my voice and showering me graciously with their writing wisdom. I am not one to forget where I have come from, and the platform you have provided I will forever be grateful for.

I would also not feel complete without thanking my parents. Dad and Mom, thank you for letting me be me. A strong-willed independent thinker from the beginning, you never stifled me, but let me run with my passions and always supported me. Thank you for taking endless hours off work to watch the girls while I wrote, and believing in this project right from the start.

And finally . . . YOU, my readers. Even on my most tired newborn mornings or toddler trying days, I open my computer at the end of the day and see you. I love hearing your success stories, helping you through your recipe firsts and seeing those sweet baby faces with runny yolks dripping off their chins! You are a joy to communicate with, and the real-ness of this movement to get kids excited about real food truly comes alive through you. Thank you for your support in this vision.

about the author

Renee Kohley is a wife and momma of 3, and she is the vision behind Raising Generation Nourished (raisinggenerationnourished.com). She grew up right in the middle of the low-fat, low-calorie "Standard American Diet" era, and after years of healing her own health issues with whole foods and lifestyle changes, a passion grew in her to see the next generation of kids grow up healthier, to love real food and know where it comes from.

Renee has spent years developing a manageable method for starting babies and toddlers with solid foods that create broad taste palates, leading to great eaters and less pickiness. Her real-world approach incorporates whole, traditional foods that nourish growing bodies without spending endless time in the kitchen fixing separate meals for kids and adults. She and her family live in Grand Haven, Michigan.

index